CLASSIC WALKS

OF NEW ZEALAND

CRAIG POTTON

CRAIG
POTTON
PUBLISHING

Text and photographs (except where otherwise credited): Craig Potton.
Project coordinator: Robbie Burton.
Editing, additional writing and track notes: David Chowdhury.
Maps: Jo Williams, Nimbus Advertising.
Layout and production: Tina Delceg.
Filmwork: Printgroup, Wellington Ltd.
Printing: Everbest Printing Co., China.

Published by Craig Potton Publishing, Box 555, Nelson, New Zealand.
©1997 Craig Potton Publishing.

First printed 1997
Reprinted 1998,1999,2000,2002.
©credited photographers.

ISBN 0 908802 39 0 (softcover)
ISBN 0 908802 43 9 (hardback)

Land Information New Zealand Map Licence PL098296/3.

CONTENTS

ACKNOWLEDGEMENTS

Many people help make a book of this nature and I'd like to give personal thanks to the staff of Craig Potton Publishing: Robbie Burton, David Chowdhury, Tina Delceg and Noleen Campbell for logistical and production work; Richard Potton, Neil Bennett, Di Dale and Rob Brown for doing the hard sell; Arnott Potter and Belinda Strickland for ensuring the book is distributed around the country. I must also thank all the Department of Conservation staff who over the years have given advice and special help, including Peter Lowen and his team on Stewart Island, Desirae Cameron at the Stratford Field Centre, Egmont National Park, Dave Rothschild at Ohakune, Tongariro National Park and the women at the DoC visitor centre beyond Murupara who told Scott and me that it often rains in the hills; John Davies, and Bill and Jackie Davidson of Routeburn Walks Ltd, Bill Nielson, Robert Romauch and the hut teams on the Milford Track.

I realise now my text is greatly lacking for not overtly acknowledging the value of close companions when out tramping. I have been very lucky to have had Andy Dennis, Beverly Potton, David Chowdhury, Derek Shaw and Rob Brown with me on several of these walks, and a special heartfelt thanks to Scott Freeman who came along on most.

Lastly, I would like to thank Andy Dennis for allowing me to use two brief extracts from unpublished material in my essays on the Heaphy and Abel Tasman tracks.

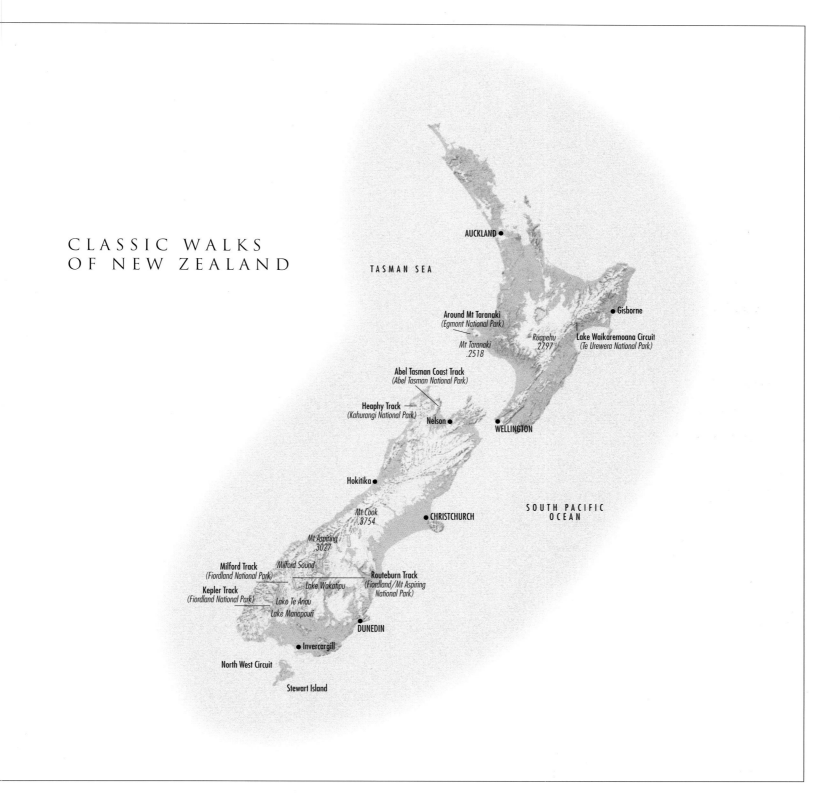

CLASSIC WALKS
OF NEW ZEALAND

TASMAN SEA

AUCKLAND •

Around Mt Taranaki
(Egmont National Park)

Mt Taranaki
.2518

Ruapehu
.2797

• Gisborne

Lake Waikaremoana Circuit
(Te Urewera National Park)

Abel Tasman Coast Track
(Abel Tasman National Park)

Heaphy Track
(Kahurangi National Park)

Nelson •

WELLINGTON

Hokitika •

Mt Cook
3754

SOUTH PACIFIC
OCEAN

• CHRISTCHURCH

Mt Aspiring
3027

Milford Track
(Fiordland National Park)

Milford Sound

Routeburn Track
(Fiordland/Mt Aspiring
National Park)

Kepler Track
(Fiordland National Park)

Lake Wakatipu

Lake Te Anau

Lake Manapouri

DUNEDIN

• Invercargill

North West Circuit

Stewart Island

INTRODUCTION

I have long wished to produce a book that celebrates walking in the New Zealand wilderness. Forests, mountain ranges, rivers and the coast have been a second home for my imagination ever since my adolescence in Nelson when, with close friends, I began exploring the back country and discovered a world that not only delighted me but was also much in need of our active care and attention. Natural landscapes speak to us with a powerful voice, and over the years, I have become convinced that the mere act of walking in nature is wonderfully therapeutic. On multi-day tramps, for reasons I can't explain, I find the rhythms of the wild soothe many of my anxieties—I think clearer and sleep with fewer demons knocking on the door of my mind.

I am aware that in producing this book I am being party to the overcrowding of these exquisite places, and the destruction of their space and solitude. However, I can also empathise with the insight of the painter Colin McCahon who described our wilderness as a "land with too few lovers". In bringing these places home to the living room I hope that an image of the wild or unfamiliar will lead to a thought that triggers a memory, creates an abstract joy and spurs us to get out once more into nature. I'm sure it is our hearts that lead our heads to such places, and our memories and desires that send us back again and again.

It has not been my intention to produce a guide that explains routes and human or natural history in any great detail. There are many other good publications that focus on these goals, and my aim is, through photos and words, to describe what I see and feel on these walks, and evoke a feeling about these places that we can all value (with the occasional diversion into scientific or personal anecdotes behind the vista).

What walks to choose for this book? There are thousands of kilometres of public tracks on conservation land to choose from, but just a dozen or so multi-day walks that consistently appear on everyone's list to do. Having no illusions about the severity of much of the landscape or the intensity of the weather, I have chosen nine well-known, well-constructed, and better-serviced lines through the forest, coast and mountains. There is nothing representative about the choice, and they are all relatively easy routes compared to many other tracks. They are also walks with large numbers of people using them during peak periods, and on which solutions to the problems of controlling numbers are being actively pursued so that the wilderness experiences of individual users aren't unduly compromised. Further, I

Korokoro Falls track, Lake Waikaremoana circuit, Te Urewera National Park.

would be roasted by my conscience (and friends!) if I promoted areas that remain off the beaten tracks.

There have been times at the end of a long day in the wilderness, with darkness falling, rain bucketing down and my shoulders in agony from a pack that has got heavier all day, when a hut has come into view, meaning a warm brew of sweet tea, a meal and a soft bunk. At times like this I feel (and if I don't I should) a debt of gratitude to the Department of Conservation workers who maintain these simple and austere shelters, as well as the other facilities that make it possible to experience a different milieu to the towns and cities in which we live.

Craig Potton

STEWART ISLAND'S
NORTH-WEST CIRCUIT
The mud and the sublime

Out on the north-west tip of Stewart Island, fifteen minutes up dunes of sand swathed in rare native coastal plants, sits East Ruggedy hut. Perfectly placed on the edge of a gnarled podocarp forest, it's where you might expect to find a recluse driven to the wilds by art or religion—if you love wilderness, and hunger for another sense of space and time from that of town and city, then you've reached home when you drop your pack on a bunk here. A large north-facing window leads your eye across the ocean to the floating grey-blue humps of the Fiordland mountains. Kiwis screech around at night, and walk right past you at dawn and dusk, poking their feathered rumps into the air and their beaks into the sand as they hunt for food. Walks northwards take you onto rolling hills high above coastal cliffs scissored by ocean rips and swells, while to the west a twenty-minute forest amble leads to a ridge of weather-sculpted granite that glows warm pink in the day's

last light. Caught between two ridges, an upward-sweeping canyon of sand and silent stones leads down to West Ruggedy Beach where westerly swells peel off the southern ocean in hypnotic repetition, smashing at the sand and rock of this sublime coast, and opening your mind to another dimension of nature's power.

I think of East Ruggedy hut as one of a number of special 'omega' points—end points of discovery halfway through a hard journey—that you can reach in wilderness walking. It won't matter if you've come from the southern or eastern routes around Stewart Island because by the time you've got to East Ruggedy beach you are way beyond your baptism by mud, thick in the trial, and nowhere near your deliverance. That being so it's worth lugging extra food or going hungry to stay at least two nights,

(Above) The daisy Olearia oporina, *endemic to Stewart Island.*
(Right) West Ruggedy beach.

Dense podocarp forest near East Ruggedy beach.

because here, in the centre of this long journey, there is a stillness that is worth savouring along with the natural generosity of the landscape and the flora and fauna, before you return to the sea of mud known as the north-west circuit of Stewart Island.

People laugh at the mud on Stewart Island because they have no choice. In many places the large brown-black wallows are grand enough for water buffaloes to bathe in, but hopeless to walk through. You can try tootsy-footing around the edges or plunging into the centre with frenzied commitment, but either way you'll lose. Oozing through boots, gaiters and socks, and sending forth an earthy pungent aroma, the mud will inevitably claim you. If there is a correct method to taking on the sinking mud it's in a style fashioned somewhere between the approaches previously described. Just accept the inevitable that you will become caked in mud, but remember to step lightly and carefully around the excessively large holes.

The north-west circuit is the biggest undertaking of all the walks described in this book, not only because of the mud, regularly wet weather and the basic state of the track, but because it is wise to carry at least ten days food (you can shorten this a day or two by hiring a water taxi to or from the hut up the Freshwater River). By walking long hours you could complete the circuit in as little as six or seven days, but hurrying across this wilderness forest, with its

Bull kelp on Lucky Beach.

lonely beaches and rock-strewn headlands, is counterproductive. Apart from the side trip up Mt Anglem, the route involves a series of subtle variations on repeating themes, and so the faster you travel the more subtlety blurs into sameness, whereas the slower you go the more you can appreciate local variety in a land echoing New Zealand before humans cut and burnt the forest back from the sea's edge.

Heading out from Halfmoon Bay any notion that this will be an easy trip across one long sunny beach after another, with a touch of forest in between, is soon dispelled. Although the beaches are places of respite and contemplation, and most of the huts are situated beside them, it is the forests that will engulf you for seven or eight days until you step onto the expansive sands of Mason Bay. The absence of

A wild and lonely landscape: the view south-east from Mt Anglem across Little Mt Anglem
and the north-east coast of Stewart Island.

South from Mt Anglem towards the Freshwater River, which drains east into Paterson Inlet.

beech and other common mainland trees like celery pine, kaikawaka and kowhai makes Stewart Island's forests seem dark and unfamiliar. The rusty tones of rimu (*Dacrydium cupressinum*), the conglomerate trunks of kamahi (*Weinmannia racemosa*), sprawling southern rata (*Metrosideros umbellata*), and the solid scalloped and flaking trunks of miro (*Prumnopitys ferruginea*) and other podocarps, in such density, invoke a sombre feeling, especially in heavy rain when even at midday it feels like the hour is late. At its

East Ruggedy hut.

margins the forest throws out strange surprises on exposed coastal fringes, with large groves of leafy wind- and salt-tolerant shrubs such as *Olearia* and *Brachyglottis*, or tight spiny-leaved shrubs of *Dracophyllum*. However, after a few

days wandering through mud bogs and up and down over tree roots you come to accept these darker colours and revel in the enclosing feel of this massive forest. In fact if you don't come to terms with this new milieu (and on our trip we met several who didn't) it's best to retreat to the pub at Halfmoon Bay.

Going north-west from Halfmoon Bay involves two days along a winding forest track, broken by interludes on beaches (the two larger being Big Bungaree and Murray), before Christmas Village is reached. On these first days are subtle signs of past human efforts to subdue the land: at Port William the buried ribs of a bygone boat, at Murray Beach the remnants of a steam traction engine from timber milling days, and beyond the beach a track following the straight line of a loggers' tramway. But a sense of 'apartness' on the north-west circuit is already well embedded in your soul by the time you have to make the decision whether or not to climb Mt Anglem from Christmas Village.

Unless it's raining the three to four hour (one way) haul up the boggy track to the rolling summit of Mt Anglem is well rewarded. Towards the end of the afternoon, light slants across an enormous land and seascape of true wilderness now rare on earth; the only hints of human habitation may be a fishing boat dwarfed by ocean swells, or the trail of smoke from the aluminium smelter at Bluff, fifty or so kilometres north on mainland New Zealand. Although just

980 metres above sea level, the feeling of being on a high mountain in a far-away place is accentuated by snow tussocks and mountain herbfields full of yellow-flowering bog lilies (*Bulbinella gibbsii*), which are at their peak in November, and Mount Cook buttercups (*Ranunculus lyallii*) in wet depressions alongside granite slabs that lie over the peat like megalithic ruins. About 400 metres beneath the summit to the south-east and south-west, two alpine tarns sit in a green and reddish sea of leatherwood (*Olearia colensoi*), and the distinctive pineapple-leaved shrubs of *Dracophyllum menziesii*. The descent is a magical walk through dense forests of leatherwood and manuka (*Leptospermum scoparium*); long strips of exfoliated manuka bark carpet the ground, creating an eerie monochromatic hue broken only by outcrops of green *Gahnia* and other grasses, and small ground-hugging ferns. Around Christmas Village I noticed an abundance of birdlife far greater than I have experienced recently on the North and South Islands; not just the common forest birds like bellbirds, tui, fantails, pigeons and tomtits, but also flocks of chattering parakeets in numbers I can remember twenty years ago in the beech forests of Nelson Lakes. Birds seemed to be finding sufficient protected nesting sites and food on Stewart Island to survive despite the obvious presence of introduced cats, white-tailed deer and possums. After a day in the bush seeing forest birds, it was a delight to discover yellow-eyed penguins on the small gravel beach beside Yankee River hut. Little blue, Fiordland crested and yellow-eyed penguins all frequent the beaches of Stewart Island, and it's not uncommon to see yellow-eyeds porpoising beyond the surf chasing schools of fish.

Granite pinnacle on the shores of Long Harry Beach.

The journey into the heart of the north-west corner begins with a hard grind up the ridge behind Yankee River hut. From now on every new place seems a little wilder and farther away from the warmth of home than you might be used to. Against a 'Japanese garden' backdrop of windswept manuka trees and bonsai

rimus, the Smoky Beach sand-dunes carry one of New Zealand's purer stands of pingao (*Desmoschoenus spiralis*), an indigenous sandbinding plant. Smoky Creek, wide and tannin-stained, hastens through dunes at the north-western end of the beach where dotterels, fairy terns, shags and penguins stand in stoic groups against the wind-driven rain.

Smoky Beach and the natural granite sculptures on the shoreline below Long Harry hut are the highlights of this remote coast before you cross the Cave Point headland and turn west into the Ruggedy beaches and East Ruggedy hut. A rest day here allows time to wander around the Ruggedys without a heavy pack, read, drink copious cups of tea and gather your reserves for the hard tramp that follows over the Ruggedy Range to Hellfire Pass hut. The crossing takes at least three hours with regular submergences in the swamps and mud in the forests above Freshwater Basin. Then the track climbs over a saddle and descends to Waituna Beach through a corridor of coastal tree daisies (the ubiquitous white-petalled and purple-centred *Olearia oporina* which is endemic to the island). Waituna Beach's northern coastal cliffs appear as if they've been spewed from the earth's molten interior just yesterday and coagulated overnight into brilliant yellow and unnaturally blue metallic clays. Beyond paua-laced rock pools and the waves sits Codfish Island, a

(Left) Evening light strikes the expansive, wind-sculpted dunelands of Mason Bay.

Pingao, the native sandbinder, enfolds a dune at Mason Bay.

scientific reserve and home to New Zealand's rarest bird, the kakapo, a large flightless parrot.

From Waituna Beach the trail climbs for several hours until at last you arrive at Hellfire Pass hut on top of an extraordinarily long and high sand-dune. Driven by the constant westerly winds that are funnelled into the vicinity of Foveaux Strait, huge layers of sand have crossed open reaches like Mason Bay—though only at Hellfire Pass does a dune rise so high and free of a substantial cover of vegetation throughout its length. It is a place of superb vistas, and as the sun sets the sweep of Mason Bay in the distance is enclosed by the darkening blue granite mounds of the Mt Allen massif, Doughboy Hill, and dotting westwards into the ocean, the Ernest Islands.

Rata and rimu forest above Paterson Inlet's North Arm (Andris Apse).

Hellfire Pass hut to Mason Bay is yet another solid five to seven hours in forest and mud broken only by the respite offered along the sands of Hellfire Beach. Mason Bay is a world unto itself—a huge expanse (described as "space illimitable" by Guthrie-Smith, an early European writer) moulded by sahara dunes coated in introduced marram grass, the native sandbinder pingao, and a succession of plants from shrubs to tall forest and even mountain tussocks on the dunes farthest inland. It's a place to wander nowhere slowly; wind sweeps sand away from shallow chasms leaving strange moonscapes of clay and small pebbles and stones placed like marbles in v-formations. Pingao roots, stems and leaves bind and surround six-metre peaked dunes, then appear to die back into hairy black skeletons as the sand moves on. Long walks on the beach to the north lead to a boulder bank of wave-smoothed rocks, while to the south is a narrow inlet between the main beach and the Ernest Islands. Huge southerly swells pulse waves through the eye of this enclosure, named appropriately, and without sentiment, 'The Gutter'. Within just 100 metres are high sea cliffs, a

(Right) Arching corridors of manuka on the track between Mason Bay and Freshwater Landing.

Twisted rata stump, blechnum ferns on the forest floor, and tree ferns, in forests near East Ruggedy hut.

delicate shell-strewn beach, another wave-lashed boulder bank, and a shipwreck in the final stages of disintegration.

From Mason Bay the north-west circuit departs the western beaches and turns inland towards Paterson Inlet where, from Freshwater Landing hut (a day's walk), you can catch a water taxi to Halfmoon Bay. Freshwater Landing is a few kilometres up the navigable Freshwater River and you arrive here having spent a relatively gentle five hours walking across swamp and tussock, and then through earthy yet ethereal corridors of manuka. If you forgo the water taxi to complete the circuit on foot, your first bath in about ten days is still another two days' walk from the landing, firstly over the Thompson Ridge to Paterson Inlet's North Arm, a strenuous eleven-kilometre trek. Here the circuit joins the Rakiura 'Great Walk' (a shorter three day orbit of north-eastern Stewart Island that also originates and ends at Halfmoon Bay). The final day to civilisation is spent on the Great Walk which passes various bays of historical note until you reach Kaipipi Bay where the trail connects with the old Kaipipi road to Halfmoon Bay.

Manuka forest at Smoky Beach planed smooth by the persistent winds that blow in from Foveaux Strait.

Storm clouds over West Ruggedy Beach.

NORTH-WEST CIRCUIT

Stewart Island

Length: 125 kilometres (full circuit); 102 kilometres if boat is caught at Freshwater Landing. Other shorter options possible.

Time required: 10-12 days (full circuit).

Nearest town: Halfmoon Bay.

Best time to walk the track: (November to March).

Fitness: good fitness is required.

A long, arduous and muddy trek, the North-west Circuit requires good fitness and equipment, bushcraft and survival skills, and weather-reading, river-crossing and navigation experience. The first and last days of the circuit are along the Rakiura 'Great Walk' which features a higher standard of facilities than the rest of the route. Hut tickets are required and camping is possible though somewhat limited. Take your own cooking equipment and utensils. All huts have fireplaces. Halfmoon Bay has a general store and accommodation. Regular flights (from Invercargill) and ferry services (from Bluff) operate between Halfmoon Bay and the South Island. The weather is unpredictable and no one period could reliably be said to be better than another. Despite the island's reputation however, it does enjoy long periods of settled weather!

Approximate track times (anticlockwise direction):

Halfmoon Bay to Port William hut (30 bunks): 4 hours.

Port William to Big Bungaree Beach hut (20 bunks): 3 hours.

Bungaree to Christmas Village hut (20 bunks): 5 hours.

Christmas Village to Yankee River hut (20 bunks): 6 hours.

Yankee River to Long Harry hut (6 bunks): 5-6 hours.

Long Harry to East Ruggedy hut (20 bunks): 3-4 hours.

East Ruggedy to Hellfire Pass hut (20 bunks): 7 hours.

Hellfire Pass to Mason Bay hut (16 bunks): 7 hours.

Mason Bay to Freshwater Landing hut (12 bunks): 3-4 hours.

Freshwater Landing to North Arm hut (30 bunks): 5-6 hours.

North Arm to Halfmoon Bay: 5 hours.

Information:

Department of Conservation,

PO Box 3, Stewart Island.

Phone: 03 219 1130. Fax: 03 219 1555.

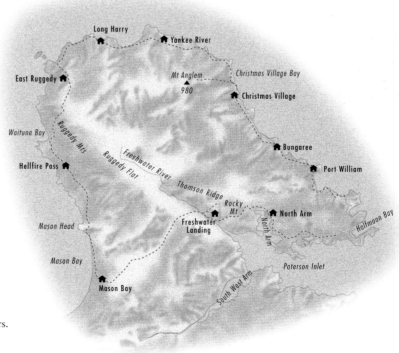

KEPLER TRACK

On the edge of the great Fiordland wilderness

Of all the classic walks in this book the Kepler is the only one that was deemed 'classic' from the moment it was conceived. Opened in 1988, it came about when the Department of Conservation joined several infrequently used routes on the Kepler Mountains into a well-constructed track, with the aim of easing the numbers of walkers crowding onto the Milford and Routeburn. That it failed in this intention and instead offered another high-standard multi-day track to walk in this wonderful part of New Zealand, was entirely predictable. But its popularity seems to prove that a track doesn't have to be an ancient Maori greenstone trail or a place of colonial history, or even feel the decades-old reverberations of explorers, hunters, trampers and their ilk to have a special poignancy in a world overwhelmed by humans.

The Kepler Track is well conceived, cuts a daring line across some spectacular Fiordland tops, and links many disparate natural features: caverns of limestone, meadows of alpine plants, forests of lowland beech and two lakes of monumental size. Furthermore, it neatly returns to its start at Te Anau like a giant uruboros (the serpent of creation that swallowed its own tail) having led you out across a wild edge of Fiordland. It takes between three and four days to walk its sixty-seven kilometres, and can be done clockwise, or, as described here, anti-clockwise.

From Te Anau to Brod Bay the Kepler starts out gently enough through a forest of red beech (*Nothofagus fusca*) and mountain beech (*N. solandri* var. *cliffortioides*) on the edge of Lake Te Anau, the largest of the South Island's lakes. Whether you wander in silence or converse with a companion, these first kilometres help to clear the mind of the recent hectic past and other unnecessary thoughts for the wilderness ahead. The harder work begins with the climb up the north-facing hill from Brod Bay to the bushline through an entrancing forest covered in lichens. When you glance into these masses of lichen they seem like

(Above) Mountain beech. (Right) Sidling around Mt Luxmore.

complete universes in themselves. Darting between these mini-worlds are diminutive head-bopping and chereeping riflemen, along with bellbirds, tomtits, warblers and parakeets. After almost an hour of steady climbing is a limestone rampart over 200 metres long and 60 metres high, that appears like a huge rippling wave frozen in the forest. This is a good place to catch your breath and contemplate the millions of years it took to form this incredible natural structure. Beyond here is the bushline where open tussock ridges lead to the over-built forty bunk edifice of Luxmore hut, high above Lake Te Anau. The tops are expansive and lie at an easy gradient, and all around are great stretches of water, mountains and sky.

When the weather is good it's worth heading down the side track close to Luxmore hut to explore the limestone cave nearby. Sloping into the hillside like an obliquely angled bullet hole, it remains about the same diameter, shape and ruler-straight gradient for at least several hundred metres, which was as far as I went with a fading torch. From the cave I wandered a short distance north across yellow-gold tussocks to look down onto the South Fiord of Lake Te Anau and up into the main reach of the lake itself. It was a view of enormous peace and grandeur, and as the evening lengthened and long stretching bands of sunlight were lost

(Left) Silver and mountain beech forest on the descent into the Iris Burn valley.

Brod Bay.

to the forests, the lake's shimmering waters became bathed in beautiful washes of hazy blues. That lakes appear in dreams as symbols of our vast unconsciousness is perhaps why they are so peaceful to our conscious mind—it's as though the act of gazing across water enables us to step through a dark door in our heads and drown our worries in its larger undercurrents. Even smaller bodies of water hold surprises as I discovered looking down onto tumbled ridges of beech forest amongst which numerous small kettle lakes visible only from above played point and counterpoint games with my mind's eye, causing the intervening ridges to pop up and down in optical riddles like an artwork by Escher.

The next day from Luxmore hut is spent almost entirely above the bushline winding around easily travelled

A speargrass mosaic on Mt Luxmore.

mountain faces and ridges. The track zigzags a few times, then climbs gradually before commencing a long sidle under the northern faces of Mt Luxmore. The rocks around Mt Luxmore sparkle with crystals and mica, their grainy and gritty texture splashed in strong dark reds and blue greys. They tend to break into large blocks, unlike the finer slates and shingles that characterise schist and greywacke mountains in the rest of the Southern Alps, and on certain outcrops form natural ruins like a stonemason's cast-offs. Many of these are 'plutonic' rocks that have been formed underground from molten rock and which have cooled extremely slowly, forming very large crystals in the process. The most unusual rocks are an *ultramafic* suite rich in magnesium and iron minerals such as dunite, an olive green

rock found on the eastern slopes of Mt Luxmore. Indeed the Kepler Track, of all the walks described in this book, is the one for those most interested in geology. Here it's possible to point to the ground and roll your tongue knowingly around such expressive words as gabbro, dunite, pegmatite, diorite and gneiss. (For excellent geological information see *A Guide to the Kepler Track* by J. Forsyth, I. Turnbull, B. Lee and G. Beecroft.)

This second day, no matter what the weather (the track is well marked with two solid shelters if the weather is bad), will etch long-lasting images into your memory. When you look down to place your feet you will see rocks and alpine

Across the Kepler tops.

tussocks, flowering herbs and mountain grasshoppers, and when you look out you will see huge Fiordland vistas, and

Sunrise golds shine on tussock grasslands above the South Fiord of Lake Te Anau. The peak opposite on the Murchison Mountains is Mt Owen.

may even experience an almost vertiginous feeling of spaciousness. On a fine day the view south, west and north is across a sprawling sea of mountains that reach out to the horizon line like wave upon wave of ocean swells. But if the weather is stormy, anxiety and awe will create a fine line between the joy of being in such an exposed situation and your necessary concern to keep warm and on track.

Invariably, a full day on the tops leaves you thirsty, hungry, and either hot or cold (I'm sure it's possible to feel both at once when you're tired), so it is a welcoming feeling when the track leaves the tops and cuts down steeply into the comfort of the subalpine forest towards the Iris Burn hut. Shrubby groves of aromatic celery pines, or toatoa (*Phyllocladus alpinus*), and bog and pygmy pines lead you into a lichen-encrusted mountain and silver (*N. menziesii*) beech forest. Further down the understorey is composed of prickly swathes of shield fern (*Polystichum vestitum*), while orchards of mountain ribbonwood (*Hoheria lyallii*) thrive on open slips. Vistas through the forest from creek crossings and slip sites give views into large sections of the broad, steepsided Iris Burn valley. From Iris Burn hut it is just twenty minutes upstream, through a dense and mossy forest of ribbonwood and giant silver beech, to where the Iris Burn River tumbles over a bluff into a wide pool, next to which an enormous fallen trunk conveniently provides a place for an evening meditation in this beautiful spot.

By making an early start the following day you can walk all the way to Rainbow Reach carpark (allow seven to eight hours), or to the Te Anau outlet in ten to eleven hours. But most prefer the five to six hour stroll down the Iris Burn to spend a third night at Moturau hut on the shores of Lake Manapouri. After the enormity of the elements and views of the day before it's a respite to walk in the enveloping warmth and security of tall beech forest—that is until about forty-five minutes downstream, when an opening, named without poetry as 'the big slip of 1984', is reached after a short climb over a moraine hill where groves of ribbonwood and leathery-barked fuchsia trees (*Fuchsia excorticata*) create elfin interludes. The slide is a sobering reminder that even the forest and its seeming security is just a graceful veneer over a turbulent landscape. During a period of exceptionally heavy rain in 1984, gravels and larger rocks from the obvious scar on the hillside across the river were strewn over the valley by a land slip. If you multiply this occurrence up and down this valley and then through every similar valley in Fiordland, then in geological terms you'll perceive the inadequacy of post-Shakespearian clichés about this "all too solid earth". All nature is in flux, but its timescale is much longer than our lives and we witness only occasional glimpses into its continuing dynamism.

(Right) The foamy veil of the Iris Burn falls cascades through beech forest close to Iris Burn hut.

The Hidden Lakes fill old glacial hollows between ridges of beech near the junction of the South Fiord and the main reach of Lake Te Anau.

After the slip you enter again the filtered light-green beech forest, the walk being broken occasionally by smaller slips, stream fans and ferny gullies. Just as your pack begins feeling as though it's as heavy as it was on the first day, the track crosses the gravels of the Iris Burn Delta, and with the hut only forty-five minutes away, you can rest by Lake Manapouri and look south across the water to the granite form of Mt Titiroa.

Beyond Moturau hut a boardwalk stretches out above a superb kettle bog, a soggy mire where tiny purple bladderworts, deep-blue swamp orchids and diminutive sundews waver amongst rustling wires of rush and green sphagnum moss. Beyond the swamp's edges kahikatea (*Dacrycarpus dacrydioides*), rimu and matai (*Prumnopitys taxifolia*) poke above the beech canopy, but in the stagnant water-laden soils of the mire these species can only grow in stunted forms. After several swamps are traversed the trail reaches the Waiau River where, at the Rainbow Reach bridge, you can catch (in summer) a shuttle bus to Te Anau; otherwise the track continues for a further three hours of forest and riverside walk to complete the circle back at Te Anau.

Forward Peak, north-west of Mt Luxmore between the track and South Fiord.

Red and silver beech forest in the Iris Burn valley.
(Left) An Iris Burn cascade.

On the shores of Lake Manapouri at Moturau Bay (Pat Barrett).

KEPLER TRACK

Fiordland National Park

Length: 67 kilometres.

Time required: 3-4 days.

Nearest town: Te Anau.

Best time to walk the track: November-April.

Fitness: moderate fitness required.

Information:

Fiordland National Park Visitor Centre,

Lake Front Drive,

PO Box 29. Te Anau.

Phone: 03 249 7924. Fax: 03 249 7613.

A Department of Conservation 'Great Walk', the Kepler Track is constructed to a high standard and has three huts with bunks, mattresses, running water and flush toilets. Heating, gas cooking facilities and coal are supplied between late October and mid April. Your own cooking equipment will be required at other times of the year. In winter through to late spring the tops are snow-covered. Camping is only possible at Brod Bay and at Iris Burn Hut. Shuttle services are available from Te Anau to and from the track, or else allow about 45 minutes to walk to the track start from Te Anau. Because this route involves a day on the tops good equipment and knowledge of weather and mountain navigation is required.

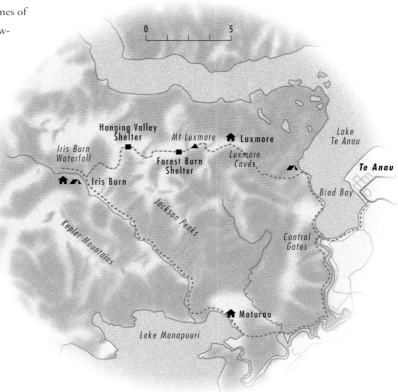

Approximate track times (anticlockwise direction):

Control Gates to Brod Bay: 1.5 hours.

Brod Bay to Mt Luxmore hut

(40 bunks): 3.5 to 4.5 hours.

Mt Luxmore hut to Iris Burn hut

(40 bunks): 5 to 6 hours.

Iris Burn hut to Moturau hut (40 bunks): 5 to 6 hours.

Moturau hut to Rainbow Reach: 1.5 hours.

Rainbow Reach to Control Gates: 2.5 to 3.5 hours.

MILFORD TRACK

In the presence of water

Fiordland is severe country with an uncompromising climate, which makes the Milford Track all the more remarkable for the relative ease with which it conveys people into the heart of this rugged wilderness. Not that walking the Milford Track is an effortless undertaking, it's more that the Milford's well-constructed path belies Fiordland's severity as it comfortably steers trampers along two immense glaciated valleys and over a high pass within a spectacular landscape of mountains, snowfields and deep-green forests. In effect, walkers of the Milford are granted all the rewards of tramping in this exceptional mountain area, yet spared the struggles that will be had in most other Fiordland valleys.

What many aren't spared walking the Milford is wet weather—it rains frequently (on average between seven and ten metres a year) and torrentially, rapidly transforming the landscape as waterfalls formed in an instant career down previously blank rock faces, gentle watercourses become seething torrents, and water flows across the valleys taking everything in its path like the mythical Assyrian army. Water is thus a dominant motif on the Milford, although not one that should deter because from safe bridges the experience of a Fiordland storm can be as exhilarating as the stupendous vistas that can be expected of a fine day. Beyond the immediate and awe-inspiring effects of a Fiordland inundation, water also works in more subtle ways, sustaining the luxuriant coatings of moss and epiphytes in its forests, and filling the pools, cascades and waterfalls that have added so much character to the Clinton and Arthur valleys. The walls of these two valleys were carved by gigantic ice age glaciers of frozen water, and even today frozen snow released in mammoth winter avalanches continues to alter the landscape and vegetation. That water is a major theme on the Milford is dramatically confirmed by the 580 metre Sutherland Falls, the biggest waterfall in New

(Above) Cruising down Lake Te Anau, on the Tawera.
(Right) Mackinnon Pass, the high point of the Milford Track, below Mt Hart, with the Clinton valley left, and the Arthur valley right.

*Beech forest overhangs peaceful pools in the Clinton River's
north branch, upstream of Clinton Forks.*

Zealand and possibly the fifth highest in the world, and also by the fact that the track is unique in this country for having to be reached by a passage across two large water masses: Lake Te Anau and Milford Sound.

During the Milford 'season' (usually between late October and mid-April) the track is always walked over four days from Lake Te Anau to Milford Sound. Along with the logistics of simply getting to this distant corner of the country, huts must be booked and transport to and from the track arranged in advance—several degrees more organisation than that required for most other walks in this book. But from Glade wharf on Lake Te Anau all that passes into memory as you wander easily up the lower Clinton valley alongside the clear deep pools of the Clinton River. Inside

this quintessential South Island forest of moss-draped red and silver beech, robins and tomtits make delicate appearances and the whole valley is alerted to your presence by the strange calls of paradise ducks and the noisy wing-thumping departures of startled wood pigeons. Moving at an easy pace it takes about two hours to reach Clinton Forks where the river branches west and north, and the mountains rise in deep-blue complement to the pale sky and the shining green forest foliage.

Clinton Forks hut is the first night's shelter for independent walkers, but no matter whether you're staying or going on towards Lake Mintaro, the forks is a good place to stop to pay homage to the creators of this 110-year-old track: Quintin Mackinnon and Donald Sutherland. In 1888

The path up the Clinton valley.

Mackinnon and Sutherland were commissioned to cut a trail that would link Lake Te Anau to Milford Sound which could only be reached by sea. With Sutherland working from the Arthur valley, Mackinnon, accompanied by Ernest Mitchell, set off up the Clinton and worked for three weeks in virtually unremitting rain and misery before crossing Mackinnon Pass on October 17, 1888. At a river beach in the Arthur valley they cooked and ate a blue duck, not in celebration but to assuage a gnawing hunger. Then, after stumbling onto the track cut by Sutherland as far as Sutherland Falls, they made their way to Milford Sound. Mackinnon returned over the pass a few days later, once again in appalling weather. Unbowed by the experience he remained in the area and established himself as the track's first guide until his untimely drowning in Lake Te Anau in 1892. Sutherland lived in Milford Sound where his wife Elizabeth ran an accommodation house for the increasing numbers of tourists participating in the fashionably new recreation of forest and mountain walking. It's difficult to know if either man quite realised how favoured their route would become, but its future popularity was assured when in 1908 photographs and articles appeared in the London *Spectator* boldly proclaiming the Milford Track "the finest walk in the world".

(Left) Mt Elliot dominates the view north of Mackinnon Pass on the descent to Quintin hut.

The immensity of Fiordland landscape is truly felt beyond Clinton Forks on the second afternoon's walk to either Pompalona or Mintaro huts in the upper reaches of

On the climb to Mackinnon Pass from the Clinton valley.

the Clinton's west branch. After the tranquillity of the lower Clinton, the landscape has an austere beauty which is accentuated when the harsher afternoon light plays on huge scarred faces of rock. Further on the dark trees of the 'black forest' (a pure stand of tall and twisted silver beech) presage a landscape desolated time and again by landslips and avalanches. Ducks quack from amongst drowned trees in a lake formed by a rockfall, while adventurous colonising plants such as wineberry (*Aristotelia serrata*), ribbonwood (*Hoheria glabrata*), flax (*Phormium tenax*), toe toe (*Cortaderia* sp.) and the prickly mountain holly (*Olearia ilicifolia*) spread out across the scenes of devastation. Despite this new

Sutherland Falls thunders into the Arthur valley.

growth, the long shadow of next winter's avalanches hangs over any confident assertions of life.

With the prospect of the climb up to Mackinnon Pass in the morning, the night spent at Mintaro or Pompalona may well have an element of wakeful self-doubt, in contrast to the confident hoots of moreporks and occasional screeching of weka, or even kiwi. All things pass however, and having roused yourself for the day ahead you are quickly lifted into another world where groves of ribbonwood spray white petals across the lower track, and stunted beech trees are draped in more moss, it would seem, than their own mass. Zigzagging easily up under the near vertical bluffs of Mt Balloon the track climbs into herbfields containing the ubiquitous Mount Cook buttercup to reach the 1,073 metre pass. Marking the summit is a surreal concrete and rock cairn emblazoned with the strange notation that it was put there in remembrance of Mackinnon by none other than the Gaelic Society and the Otago Rugby Union (Mackinnon was an outstanding rugby player), with the help of the New Zealand government. If the day is clear, a fifteen minute walk towards Mt Balloon takes you away from your fellow walkers, though sadly never far enough away from the alienating buzzing roar of aeroplanes and helicopters. Below lies the tarn-spotted pass, and beyond is Mt Hart, its ridges carving and splitting into monstrous mountain cul-de-sacs. To the right, under the precariously sloped ice-shelf of the

New Zealand's native tomtit.

Jervois Glacier, a series of waterfalls pour down Mt Eliot's fluted rock face.

For some, the long descent off the pass into the Arthur valley brings a painful awareness of knees and ankles, and a reminder that the ascent of any high pass or mountain is just half the journey. Inevitably though the track crosses Roaring Creek to first reach Quintin, and then Dumpling hut. After a rest, and despite the anger in your legs, the two kilometre side trip from here to Sutherland Falls is obligatory because not only are the falls truly awe-inspiring, but even the track's tunnel of glowing red-gold fuchsia, dark-green shield ferns, beech trees and tree ferns (*Cyathea smithii*) are enough to compel you forward. As you stand beneath the mesmeric leaps of water picture William Quill, who in

1890 climbed the sheer wall immediately beside these falls and at the top discovered the lake that now bears his name.

The final day in the Arthur valley leads down the line of Sutherland's old track to Milford Sound, and soon reaches one of the most picturesque spots on the Milford Track: Bell Rock. From here you look into Mackay Falls, a scene that is resplendent with power and grace in heavy rain. In

Luxuriant coatings of moss draped over sprawling beech limbs in the Arthur valley.

contrast to this more conventional beauty the track crosses numerous areas wrecked by landslides and rockfalls. Though these eerie scenes reek of dead plants and shattered rocks, rockfalls are a necessary cycle in Fiordland's valleys for they restore minerals to soils leached by the vast amount of rain that falls here every year. About 1,000 years ago a huge

rockfall dammed the river and formed Lake Ada in the lower Arthur. When the lake's level is low tree stumps litter the surface, a collection of decaying sentinels speaking silently of an earlier time.

With a boat to catch from Sandfly Point on the last afternoon, and an awareness that this was the last day of a great trip, my mind wandered more frequently than usual beyond my footfalls on the path and the present moment. It occurred to me that the Milford Track itself is a path of history through the natural world. Although it is a restrained imprint, rocks nonetheless have been laboriously shifted, boardwalks built over swamps, rivers bridged, and a sloping stairway dynamited out of solid rock around Lake Ada. It is nice to think that for over a hundred years now people have walked this track, enriching their imaginations and singing the praises of this precious protected landscape. The climax of the track at Milford Sound is fittingly Wagnerian in scale, with steeply angled rock faces rising sheer for thousands of metres from the dark depths of the sound. Engulfed by this scene, it is hard not to feel privileged being able to spend time journeying on tracks such as the Milford.

(Right) Surrounded by ferns and beech forest, Mackay Creek cuts deeply through the bedrock and emerges on the Milford Track at a bouldery cascade known as Mackay Falls.

Looking back into the Arthur valley from Milford Sound.

Mitre Peak, and the prominent rounded shoulder of The Lion to the right, in Milford Sound.

Giant Gate Falls, on the last day to Sandfly Point.

MILFORD TRACK

Fiordland National Park

Distance: 54 kilometres.
Time required: 4 days.
Nearest centre: Te Anau.
Best time to walk the track: November-April.
Fitness: moderate fitness required.

Information:
Fiordland National Park Visitor Centre,
Lake Front Drive,
PO Box 29, Te Anau.
Phone: 03 249 7924. Fax: 03 249 7613.

A Department of Conservation 'Great Walk', the track is constructed to a high standard. The weather can be severe and good equipment is essential. Snow can fall on Mackinnon Pass at any time of the year. All DoC huts are supplied with gas cookers, mattresses, and heating. Huts must be booked in advance between late October and April and given the popularity of this track early booking is advised. During the 'season' the track is always walked from Lake Te Anau to Milford Sound. Outside this period booking is not required, though gas facilities are removed from the huts, and at times huts are closed for maintenance. Some bridges are also removed from the path of winter avalanches. Trampers should be aware of the high avalanche risk in this area during winter and spring. There are a number of ways to reach the track from Te Anau, including float-plane, kayak and water-taxi, and similar arrangements can be made at the Milford Sound end for the return journey to Te Anau. Guided walks are also available on the Milford.

Approximate track times:
Glade wharf to Clinton Forks hut: 8.5 kilometres, 2 hours.
Clinton Forks hut to Mintaro hut: 13 kilometres, 4-5 hours.
Mintaro hut to Dumpling hut: 14 kilometres, 6 hours.
Dumpling hut to Sandfly Point: 18 kilometres, 5-6 hours.

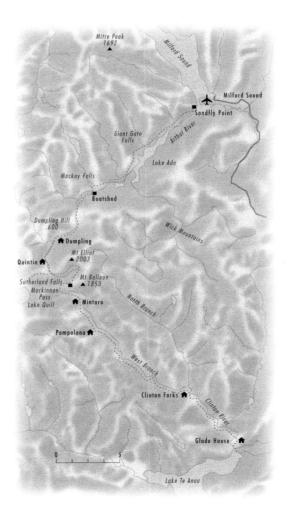

ROUTEBURN TRACK

In the aftermath of ice

The Routeburn Track is a high mountain traverse of the Ailsa and Humboldt Mountains, two spectacular glacier-sculpted sandstone ranges wedged between the granite peaks of Fiordland's Darran Mountains and the crumbling schist ranges of Mount Aspiring National Park. If you start the Routeburn from its southern end and climb to the grand viewpoint that is Key Summit, you gain almost immediately an impression of the impact glaciers had on the southern South Island landscape—in fact everywhere you look is a postscript to the last ice age that peaked 15,000 to 20,000 years ago. Below, the Hollyford valley describes the classic U-shape of a glacier-carved valley, and its steep sides retain the classical imprints of a post-glacial landscape: hanging valleys, headwalls, cirque basins and aquamarine tarns. Across the valley where remnant glaciers persist on the highest Darrans' summits, are fine glacier-honed 'arete peaks' like Pyramid and Christina, while northwards lies the beautifully rendered Emily Peak above Lake Mackenzie in the Ailsa Mountains. You can start

to comprehend the enormous drama of ice on the move that took place here if morning cloud has filled the Hollyford to the bushline, and you imagine that cloud being a huge glacier fed by numerous side glaciers. Indeed, so deep was the glacier that filled the Hollyford that it flowed over Key Summit, today a forest-fringed mountain bogland, and dispersed tongues of ice down the Eglinton and Greenstone valleys while the main flow continued down the Hollyford to well beyond the present shore at Martins Bay.

The glacial imprint appears so fresh because the granites and sandstones of which these dramatic mountains are made are more resistant to the weathering forces that have worn away the glacial record elsewhere. At any time of year, even in midsummer, walking the Routeburn can become a meditation on the language of glaciers as you move beneath sculpted faces and ridges, past lakes Howden, Mackenzie

(Above) Swingbridge over the Route Burn. (Right) Crossing Harris Saddle, going east towards Lake Harris and Mt Xenicus.

Alpine tarn and sphagnum bog on Key Summit, with Mt Christina in the Darran Mountains on the left skyline.

and Harris created when the ice melted back, and past large boulders sure to be heavily scratched and serrated by broken rocks dragged over their surfaces by ice.

Although the Routeburn can be walked in three days (with evenly spaced stops at Lake Mackenzie and Routeburn Falls), it's worth spending a second night at Lake Mackenzie and exploring the montane forest on its shores and the alpine areas beyond. From the Milford Road, and after the Key Summit turn-off, the way to Mackenzie hut continues past Lake Howden through mountain and silver beech forests, and the occasional open frosty area laid bare by avalanches and floods now graced with shield ferns and deciduous ribbonwood (the latter identifiable by its light-green foliage and white hibiscus-like flowers). In such places, even in summer, the sun seldom touches their blue shade and the creek water is so cold and fresh to drink it sears at your head. Earland Falls, a picturesque cascade ninety minutes from Lake Howden, is a delightful place to doff packs on a hot afternoon and relax amongst the sun-warmed boulders and pools below the falls.

On my first evening at Lake Mackenzie I found myself inside an archaic, chaotic and quite beautiful mountain beech forest on the lake's southern shore. I find it hard to write about the kind of visual pleasure such places impress upon me (and there are many of them in the Southern Alps!) because sensual impulses are not so easily rendered in words, and because I'm never sure if it's the pull of the place or my mood at the time that initiates the excitement. Squat, tough and bent trees, drenched in mosses and lichens, reached their roots over moss-covered glacial boulders into deeper realms of moss on the soggy forest floor. Nearby, water lapped against discordant piles of rocks, and Emily Peak and other peaks rose above the shadowed valley, glowing eerily in the evening light and standing over us, mute and muscular. I spent the next day engrossed by the forest, lake and mountain faces, wandering slowly and musing about all kinds of things—as you do when you're entranced by a world not of your making—returning more than once to some forest glades and lakeside rocks, and even the next morning returned to that first grove before turning up the zigzag path and heading for Routeburn Falls.

All the day along the Hollyford face to Harris Saddle and down to Routeburn Falls, about fifteen kilometres' walk, is spent in the alpine zone exposed to the elements, which must be in your favour before you start. Clear or even intermittently clear weather to Harris Saddle allows panoramas of the Darran Mountains, the highest of which are the blocky ramparts of Tutoko (2,746 metres) and Madeline (2,537 metres). As you walk alpine grasshoppers jump away from your feet in random springloaded leaps, and alpine tussocks and flowers unique to New Zealand waver in the constant breezes that blow across the Hollyford face.

In high summer these wide slopes are crowded with flowers, and when admiring their beauty it's also worth pondering the fact that about ninety per cent of New Zealand's mountain plants won't be found anywhere else in the world. That's because for the last 80 million years New Zealand has been geographically isolated from any other land, allowing its cargo of plants to adapt and specialise. While it seems surprising that plants survive at all in high altitudes they have done so by evolving ways to cope with the impoverished soils and harsh alpine environment found throughout New Zealand mountain areas. Most of New Zealand's alpine plants grow between the treeline and rocky screes; tussocks and sprawling shrubby plants take their place in a narrow band above the treeline and higher still are found the flowering herbs, tall and short snow tussocks, many species of sharp speargrasses, cushion plants and alpine grasses. Of the herbs the most revered are the white-flowered, glossy-leaved Mt Cook buttercup (the largest buttercup in the world), and closely related yellow buttercups. But much more numerous than the buttercups are mountain daisies from the *Celmisia* family of plants, though ourisias and gentians are also common, and the South Island edelweiss (*Leucogenes grandiceps*), recognised by its white woolly flowerhead and fuzzy silver leaves, will be found on higher

(Left) Mountain beech forest on the southern shores of Lake Mackenzie.

Sunset on Emily Peak (centre), above Lake Mackenzie.

outcrops. Boggy places like those on Key Summit and in the Harris Basin are another feature of the alpine zone. In these grow a variety of moisture-loving plants—sphagnum mosses, sundews, bladderworts, bog pines, daisies, orchids, the white caltha and the native forget-me-not *Myosotis macrantha*. Tread carefully, though preferably not at all, amongst these fragile, easily damaged boglands.

The sidle along the Hollyford face continues for about two hours before turning sharply up to Harris Saddle (1,277 metres) where there is a small A-frame shelter. When it's fine it's just 250 metres up to Conical Hill for views of extraordinary spaciousness. Eastwards, across linear glacier-smoothed slabs of tussock and rock, lies Lake Harris and the amphitheatre of scattered boulders known as the Valley of the Trolls; behind the lake a squat Mt Xenicus (an outlier of the Humboldt Mountains), Harris Basin, and way beyond, the Dart valley. To the south and west a visual line leads off the summits of Tutoko and Madeline deep into the Hollyford valley, the broad reaches of Lake McKerrow and the shimmering silver of the Tasman Sea.

It is elating and relaxing to reach a high pass in good time with all of what is left of the day to reach your next destination. Having reached Harris Saddle, the remaining journey is an easy downhill walk past Lake Harris and the rough tussock meadows of Harris Basin. If you have the time and weather to dawdle these last kilometres, twilight is a wonderful time to stroll into Routeburn Falls hut, which is set amongst dwarf beech trees near a dancing watercourse and the Routeburn Falls. The eastward facing hut site is not a place to leave too early in the morning either. Rather, get up early, make a cup of tea, sit down on the veranda and let the sun rise over the ranges beyond the Dart River to warm your tired body and lazy soul. Then share vicariously in the energy and stubborn inquisitiveness of the keas on their customary morning visit.

Rest assured the last day of the journey continues in the easy downward pace that began after lunch the day before and is largely through a beech forest that blankets you from the previous day's more raw exposure to the elements. You soon discover though when you cross the large land-slide near Falls hut, then when you pass 'the sump' in the lower Route Burn, that all is not as eternally comforting as it seems. The slip is reached not long after tall forest gains an encompassing grip on the land above Routeburn Flat. In 1994, after several days of torrential rain, the scant soils on this slope gave way and thundered toward the flat, releasing a huge quantum of energy and debris. Despite the immediate catastrophic impacts of landslides, beech forests thrive on such crises; even after a minor event such as the fall of a single tree the extra light falling through the canopy triggers strong and rapid growth in beech seedlings, which often wait years for that chance. And as can be seen around the valley where variations in the heights of trees indicate the sites of past slips and rockfalls, beech forests have been coping with crisis for thousands of years.

Order returns beyond the slip, and on a sunny day the views and containment of the tussock-covered flats where the west and north branches of the Route Burn meet take on a prelapsarian warmth, with, ironically, the only raucous discord likely to come from pairs of paradise ducks asserting their territorial demands. Back in the forest tomtits and bush robins approach with Eden-like innocence, though more than likely their interest is in snapping up any insects stirred by your footfall through the leaf litter.

'The sump'—a bottleneck of tree trunks and boulders thrust haphazardly together as if a giant had crushed his

The granite crest of the Darran Mountains, across the Hollyford valley; from near Lake Mackenzie.

The kea, New Zealand's mountain parrot.

marbles amongst his pick-up-sticks—is encountered where the track enters the top of the forested Route Burn gorge. Called 'the sump' because into this morass the river disappears, it is a place of dread and awe, yet exhilarating to stand on the edge of, knowing that the track can be regained a mere thirty metres above. In this shadowed valley, dead trees lie ripped of their bark and jammed at awkward angles, their skeletal forms shining blue, grey and cream. Somewhere around here in 1864 three prospectors, Alphonse "George" Barrington and his companions James Farrell and Antoine Simonin struggled back towards Lake Wakatipu after an epic journey of six months in the West Coast valleys of the Hollyford, Pyke and Cascade, and the lifeless Red Hills region. Living on a woefully inadequate diet of occasional kakapo, weka, robins and the like, and badly frostbitten, Barrington wrote, not without the spirit of irony and strong will that kept him going: "If fasting and praying is of any value to sinners, we ought soon to become saints". Stare into the sump, contemplate their agony and smile wryly at Barrington's indomitable wit.

In counterpoint to the gorge and the sump are the welcoming red beech trees in the last hour before the road end. Such groves create a world of green I shall never tire of, neither foreboding nor overbright, their layered leaves are an aesthetic repose after the immensity of the vistas of the last few days.

Tall red beech forest in the last kilometres to Routeburn Shelter.

An early winter fall of snow in the Route Burn valley, looking down onto Route Burn flats from near Route Burn Falls (Andris Apse).

Boulders from the landslide that dammed Lake Mackenzie lie near the lake's subterranean outlet.

The entrance to 'the sump' in the Route Burn gorge.

ROUTEBURN TRACK

Fiordland and Mount Aspiring National Parks

Distance: 32 kilometres.

Time required: 2-3 days.

Nearest centres: Glenorchy and Te Anau.

Fitness: moderate fitness required.

A high mountain traverse in Fiordland and Mount Aspiring National Parks, the Routeburn is a Department of Conservation 'Great Walk'. The mountainous terrain and exposure to bad weather means good equipment is required. There are four huts, all supplied with gas cookers, mattresses and heating. Camping is permitted next to Mackenzie and Routeburn Flats huts. Between late October and April, hut accommodation has to be booked in advance. Outside this period gas facilities are removed from the huts and your own cooking equipment will be required. In winter the track is snow-covered with risks from avalanches. The track can be walked in either direction. Guided walks are also available on the Routeburn. There are good transport services to and from the track.

Approximate track times (Milford Road to Routeburn Shelter):

The Divide to Lake Howden hut: 2 hours.

Lake Howden hut to Mackenzie hut: 3-4 hours.

Mackenzie hut to Routeburn Falls hut: 5-7 hours.

Routeburn Falls hut to Routeburn Flats hut: 30 minutes to 1 hour.

Routeburn Flats to Routeburn Shelter: 3 hours.

Information:

Queenstown Field Centre,

Department of Conservation,

PO Box 811, Queenstown.

Phone: 03 442 8916. Fax: 03 442 7932.

(Alternatively, contact the Fiordland National Park Visitor Centre, details in Milford Track chapter)

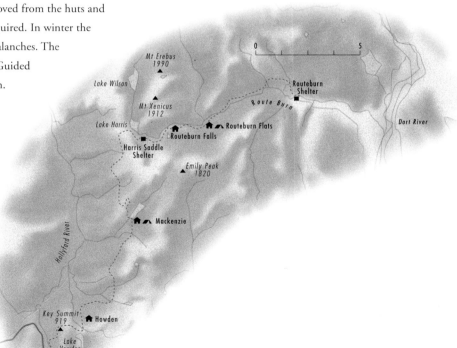

HEAPHY TRACK

Silent downs and pounding surf

Two contrasting landscapes are likely to linger in your mind after you've walked the Heaphy: one, a high silent tussock plateau, the other, a loud coastline where waves reach brashly towards groves of tropical palms and flowering rata. Experiencing these contrasts, diverging emotions and memories of fear and attraction, awe and intimacy are often accentuated—it is all part of the pull and variety you experience on this traverse through forests and ancient geological structures in the north-west of Kahurangi National Park.

Most begin the Heaphy from Brown Hut at the northern end of the trail in Golden Bay, and allow between three and five days to reach its conclusion on the West Coast. Setting out from here delegates all the climbing to the first day, leaving the easy wander along the western beaches, with considerably lightened packs, until last. Once beyond the first paddocks and scrubby spurs the track enters a diverse forest that includes huge old red and hard beeches and rimu and miro, with distinctive mikimiki (*Coprosma linariifolia*)

and toro (*Myrsine salicina*) trees in the understorey. As the zigzag climb continues the intimate feel of the forest is broken by occasional supplejack tangles and large landslips. The track is benched and follows an easy grade up the hillside along a route constructed in 1893 to allow pack horses to be moved through the area. It is thanks to those who built the track that for the first hours at least you can let your mind wander freely or disengage completely without worrying too much about where to put your feet, though you will be pulled back in lyrical moments by attentive fantails and tomtits or the distinctive calls of kaka, bellbird and tui. Streams are crossed at regular intervals and windows in the forest open towards the granite summits of the Lead Hills and Mount Olympus across the Aorere valley, and beyond to the Dragons Teeth on the Douglas Range. Major lookouts occur at the Aorere Shelter eleven kilometres from Brown River, where mountain cabbage trees

(Above) Scotts Beach.

Coastal forest on the western beaches: nikau palms, tree ferns, tall rata and clinging kiekie vines.

(*Cordyline indivisa*) protrude disjunctively, and a further three kilometres on at Flanagan's Corner. The latter, the highest point on the track, offers a first westward glance to Perry Saddle hut, about thirty minutes away.

It's worth starting early the next day before the sun banishes the moody blue cast and low mists that often lie across the Gouland Downs, about an hour's descent from Perry Saddle. When you step onto the downs you are immediately struck by the strangeness of this high rolling plateau of open tussock and occasional forest, as well as the contrast with the rustling forest of mountain neinei and silver beech encountered between Perry Saddle and the downs. Perhaps the downs landscape catches you off guard because mountainous country isn't meant to be so smooth and flattish, and forests aren't supposed to sit above alpine tussocklands. For whatever reason, it's queer country and nearly everyone feels something of its eeriness, even if only in retrospect down in the semi-tropical forests of the Heaphy valley. For those with a mind for geology the Gouland Downs, one of the oldest landforms in New Zealand, is fascinating terrain. Like the Mt Arthur Tablelands to the east and the Matiri plateaux in the south, the downs are what remains of a huge low-lying peneplain that was formed 80 to 100 hundred million years ago out of 400- to 500-

(Left) Layers of understorey trees and shrubs in the hardwood forests between Brown hut and Perry Saddle.

The giant moss Dawsonia superba.

million-year-old siltstones and sandstones. This vast peneplain eventually sank below the sea and limestone was deposited onto it before the land was raised again in the present phase of mountain building. Much of the limestone has been eroded off, revealing the old surface again which now stands over 600 metres above the sea.

Next to tussocks and light-grey skeletons of dwarfed manuka on the track's edge, tiny purple orchids bob up from the mud and gravels. With the notable exception of its fertile islands of limestone, the downs' soils have been severely leached of nutrients. Consequently this is no country for growth of any vigour other than the tussocks and alpine shrubs and flowers that have adapted to these conditions. There are many rare and endemic plants here and some, like the *Ourisia goulandiana*, as the name suggests, grow only on these downs.

Specialisations such as this, and the rarity of many plants here and elsewhere in Kahurangi influenced the course of events that led to this vast region of north-west Nelson being declared New Zealand's thirteenth national park. Geological variety and the presence of the country's oldest

The endemic North West Nelson gentian Gentiana spenceri.

landforms were other factors, along with the significance of the area for native wildlife. This western region of the park, and Gouland Downs in particular, is the stronghold for the endangered great spotted kiwi, and while you would have to be determined to sight one of these large nocturnal creatures in the wild, you will quite likely hear their screeching calls after dark. By day the flightless western weka and

spirited flocks of pipits will be the most common birds seen, and if you're very lucky, you might glimpse the diminutive fernbird whose cryptic colours allow it to merge into the rushes and tussocks.

Two to three hours from Perry Saddle is the old Gouland Downs hut and one or two hours farther the newer Saxon hut. Both are good bases for exploring the limestone outcrops, sinkholes and other features of this limestone karst (karst is a Czech term for waterworn) landscape, and also the plants of the area, which are at their flowering best in midsummer. As you move over the downs the track traverses tussock flats where rivers like the Big cut raw into the old peneplain and begin coiling and curling in slow meanders before their sudden westward plunge towards the Tasman Sea. After a steady descent into mossy beech forest near the confluence of the Saxon River and Blue Duck Creek, the geology abruptly changes. Now, on the way up to the Mackay Downs and towards Mackay hut, the ancient sedimentary rocks of the peneplain are replaced by a coarse granite that provides the rest of the track's stolid bedrock (with the exception of the dramatic limestone landscapes of the lower Heaphy valley and Kohaihai bluff). The vistas of the Mackay Downs are not as large as those of the Gouland. Instead the track weaves through a maze of tussock- and scrub-covered basins enclosed by forested hills on the side of Mt Teddy. Large yellowy-grey granite 'core stones' rise

Subalpine tussock grasslands on the Gouland Downs, looking east towards the Gouland Range.

above stunted rata, dracophyllums, mountain toatoa and manuka. Eventually Mackay hut looms on a knoll above the track and the intimacy of this country relents, satisfying a desire for wider horizons and giving a wonderful view down to the Tasman Sea at the mouth of the Heaphy River.

Mackay hut is where the Heaphy leaves the rolling downs landscape and begins its long and gradual descent into forests towards the Heaphy River and the sea. In terms of the altitude surrendered, the evenness of the gradient, the unbroken mantle of deep-green forest and the hypnotic effects of the track's gentle and endlessly repeating curves, the way between Mackay and Lewis hut is not dissimilar to the first day. However there are some differences. In the wetter western forests mosses and ferns are far more common, and rimu and rata grow more abundantly as can be expected on the West Coast. By the time Lewis hut is reached the stark austerity of the downs has been washed into memory by the luxuriance of the enveloping forest, and coastal/tropical associations blatantly manifest in the dense tangles of epiphytes and lianes, and the appearance of the first scattered nikau palms.

If tramping is a process by which sweat and toil is the price paid for entering realms where the soul is uplifted by wild nature, then (for those heading westwards) Lewis hut

(Left) Weathered granite outcrop on Scotts Beach (Rob Brown).

is where the trade-offs between effort and reward shift dramatically in favour of the latter. From here to Kohaihai the track rarely climbs more than a few metres above river level or the high tide line, and the scenery is always superb. Heading down river the track wends between exquisite avenues of nikau palms and tree ferns, and massive northern rata clear the surrounding canopy, festooned in perching and climbing plants. Kiekie and supplejack vines make much of this forest quite impenetrable, and warmth-loving species like kawakawa, rangiora and kowhai complement the forest's exotic nature. Further enhancing this section along the river's final meanders to the coast is a dramatic array of limestone landforms including a rank of bluffs that not only walls in the southern bank, but also provides intriguing trackside architecture.

Where rivers meet the sea are often places of physical and psychic power, though few carry the consistent intensity of the Heaphy River mouth just below Heaphy hut. There is almost always a large surf running hard into the river as it rushes across the swollen face of the sand. After three or four days walking the paradox in which the almost violent power of the place seems to create a sense of inner peace and contentment cannot be escaped, especially at dusk when the sun boils into the western sea behind the rising spray of breaking waves. The river mouth area—the site of a Maori settlement and seasonal camp dating to 1380 AD—

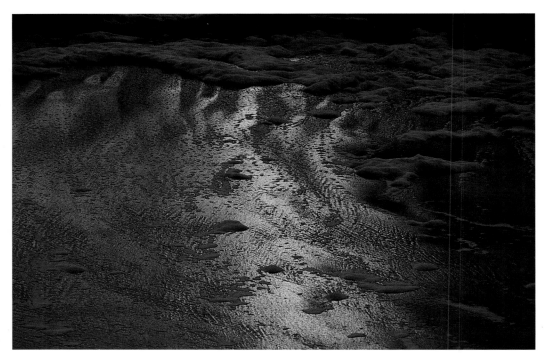

Sea foam, pushed by wind and tide onto the western beaches.

is sacred to the Ngai Tahu tribe and has been excluded from the national park. It is one of few sites in the whole of the South Island's north-west occupied by humans for any extended time, and the discovery of stone flints suggests there was once a thriving trade here in stone tools made at the camp from greenstone, argillite, chert and obsidian imported from other parts of the country.

It won't matter what the weather does on the last day from Heaphy hut to Kohaihai shelter because this is a wonderful walk in any conditions. When the weather is wild and stormy the beaches are covered with pulsing creamy foam and the sea thunders landwards from the horizon in huge sets of waves. In the rain and wind you can find quiet respite amongst groves of nikau palms, and when it's sunny and hot and the swell's not too huge, the ambience is more that of a tropical island. Across headlands and beaches the five hours to the road end can be strung out to a whole day in the knowledge that all the streams are bridged and the only major climb is the short ascent over the saddle between Scotts Beach and Kohaihai shelter, leaving you time to savour the golden sands, subtropical forest and the unceasing pounding of the surf.

Nikau forest on the coast between Kohaihai Shelter and the Heaphy River.

Foam-covered boulders on the western beaches of the Heaphy Track.
(Left) Lush rainforest flanks a side creek in the Heaphy valley.

The trunk of a giant rata in the Heaphy valley.

Nikau forest interior.

HEAPHY TRACK

Kahurangi National Park

Distance: 78 kilometres.

Time required: 4-6 days.

Nearest centres: Collingwood (Golden Bay);
Karamea (West Coast).

Best time to walk: November to April.

Fitness: moderate fitness required.

A Department of Conservation 'Great Walk', the track is
constructed to a high standard and has seven huts including Brown
hut at the Aorere valley roadend. Hut tickets are required for all
huts and camping is allowed at designated campsites. All huts
except Gouland Downs hut have gas cookers, mattresses and
heating. Carrying tents is advisable during peak months.
There are a number of shuttle bus services to either
end of the track during the summer. Light aircraft
can be chartered to enable a return to vehicles at
either end of the track.

Approximate track times (north to south
from Aorere valley, Golden Bay):

Brown hut to Perry Saddle hut (40
bunks): 16 kilometres, 5-6 hours.

Perry Saddle to Gouland Downs hut
(12 bunks): 6 kilometres, 2 hours.

Gouland Downs hut to Saxon hut
(40 bunks): 6 kilometres, 2 hours.

Saxon hut to Mackay hut (40
bunks): 12 kilometres, 3-4 hours.

Mackay hut to Lewis hut (40
bunks): 12 kilometres, 3 hours.

Lewis hut to Heaphy hut (40 bunks): 8 kilometres, 2-3 hours.

Heaphy hut to Kohaihai shelter: 16 kilometres, 4-5 hours.

Information:

Department of Conservation,

Nelson/Marlborough Conservancy,

Private Bag 5, Nelson.

Phone: 03 546 9335. Fax: 03 548 2805.

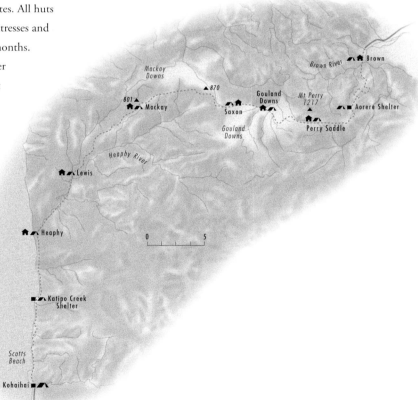

ABEL TASMAN
COAST TRACK

Meandering by the ocean

Whether you walk north or south along the Abel Tasman National Park coast track makes little difference to your encounter with this quiet coast. Within a few hours, whichever direction you go, are repeating themes of water, sand, rock and forest, and enchanting sequences of small sheltered beaches and shallow tidal inlets. In many ways the coast track is the hardest to write about yet the easiest to enjoy. It's difficult to be overly expressive or adjectival because the forest isn't continuously great (in fact there's a lot of gorse and low scrub), the track itself is so easy and repetitive (where's the challenge?), the geology consists of granite, granite and more granite, and even the beauty of the beaches is plainly self-evident. Just being on the sand induces a pleasing soporific effect—the body and mind doodle along like the track itself, stopping frequently in blank seas of blue and gold. The point is almost reached where the coast's picturesque qualities, easy access, comfortable

facilities and the degenerate state of the forest blinds you to the exceptional impact that some particular features have. Sculpted granite headlands, green beech leaves against jet black tree trunks, koru fern forms, and sunrise golds on sand ripples and ake ake trunks—all have lifted me to a high state of delight, suggesting that the coast track's greatest impact is not in its overall qualities, but in its details.

Undoubtedly the Abel Tasman coast track is the most popular multi-day track in New Zealand because of its ease (in summer you can do it in sandshoes or sandals) and its swimmable sandy beaches, fringed in places by lush vegetation and ferns that evoke a semi-tropical mood. It can be walked at any time of the year though don't be fooled by tropical appearances in winter because it gets cold at night and only the hardiest swim!

(Above) Sea-weathered granite boulders. (Right) Sunrise on Awaroa Head, Awaroa Bay.

Access too is much easier than most other New Zealand walks, with daily bus services from Nelson to Marahau, Totaranui and Wainui, and water-taxis that call at many locations along the coast. Four large huts are well situated beside the ocean and conveniently spaced along the track, while virtually every accessible beach has a campsite nestled amongst forest on foreshore dunes. Most people allow three to five days to walk the fifty kilometres of track between Marahau in the south and Wainui Bay in the north, then again shorter walks are possible by being dropped off or collected at points along the coast by water-taxi.

You appreciate almost immediately how much this park differs from all others in the scale of human modification that has occurred when you walk from Marahau over the causeway across Sandy Bay inlet. Here and elsewhere in the park whole hillsides of native forest are recovering from 100 years of clearfelling and fires—a history of destruction that came to little largely because the park's soils were too infertile for either plantations or farming, and which was also why the devastation of forests never reached its ultimate conclusion. But by the 1930s about three-quarters of the coastal landscape carried the scars of continual burning, and pines, gorse and other introduced weedy plants had spread. A number of forest reserves existed at the time and conser-

(Left) Te Pukatea Bay.

The elegant extending branches of a forest fern.

vationists and community-spirited individuals, most especially the indefatigable Perrine Moncrieff, argued that these should be combined with land purchased by government to form a national park that would allow native vegetation to recover. The national park came to be in December 1942, the beginning of an 'experiment' in landscape recovery in which the hopes of the future lay with the natural regeneration that continues today.

It is not until you turn the first major headland beyond Tinline Bay that you enter a gully and hillside of mature beech forest and experience the splendour of the tall indigenous trees that will, in time, reclothe most of this landscape. To glance through forest windows and see the grey rain-spotted ocean beyond, with Adele Island silently

Hard beech and large mamaku tree ferns near Torrent Bay.

proclaiming a darker-grey presence, is a compelling aesthetic reason for walking this coastal stretch in the rain. Trees and ferns gleam, and the blackest trunks contrast with subtle variations of iridescent green. But rainy weather is clearly not the most favourable for spending time on the beaches that regularly appear after short hillside sidles. These coves are best enjoyed in intense sun when the sky and water are so blue all other colours except the sands appear subdued and washed of their lustre.

Before the track winds down to the Anchorage campsite and hut, it cuts over a depauperate hummocky ridge where repeated burnings and virtually non-existent soils have created spasmodic groves of contorted manuka and kanuka. But even here, as everywhere in the many taller kanuka/manuka groves along the track, small native orchids raise their resplendent flowerheads in late spring and summer. From these relatively open heights is a magnificent view south into the waterway known as Astrolabe Roadstead between Adele Island and the bays towards Marahau. The many French placenames come from the navigator Dumont d'Urville, the second European to visit this coast after the Dutch explorer Abel Janzoon Tasman. In marked contrast to Abel Tasman's brief and bloody encounter with Maori somewhere off the coast west of Separation Point in 1642, d'Urville and the crew of his corvette *Astrolabe* established close links with Maori during the week they spent hove-to

in the roadstead, in January 1827. As well as conducting harmonious relations with the local people, d'Urville's visit yielded a valuable historical, scientific and artistic record of the coastline.

From the ridge high above Anchorage the view north leads through the park's central landscapes: a repeating series of crescent beaches, sandbars, shell-strewn estuaries, coves and headlands. Just as the granite beneath your feet defines the vegetation's limits, when combined with water granite becomes the main ingredient in the overall shape, colour and feel of the land. The magmatic brew that produced the park's fairly easily weathered 'exfoliating' granite is rich in quartz, feldspar and mica. Large quantities of these

Tonga Island, the focal point of the Tonga Island marine reserve, from Onetahuti Beach.

sparkling minerals have been eroded into rivers and streams and washed to the coast, where modest currents have massed them together to form coarse granite sands ranging in colour from reddish gold to brilliant white. The coastline has evolved into a series of basins carved from more yielding areas of rock between ridges of harder, more resistant rock— the result is a sequence of curvaceous indentations on an otherwise rugged and irregular coast. A large tidal range (between three and four metres between high and low tides) adds finishing touches, endlessly rearranging large quantities of colourful sands.

Anchorage hut is a good base for a day, or at least a morning, exploring the beaches at Torrent Bay, Anchorage and Te Pukatea Bay, the sculpted headlands in between, and the grainy granite blocks sitting incongruously in the river around Cleopatra's Pool, a short walk up the Torrent River. The coast track swings inland from Torrent Bay for several hours, but retains delightful views into several idyllic estuaries. (After the Falls River swingbridge it's worth sidling off to Sandfly Bay if you can spare the time.) Bark Bay, where the next major hut is located, has all the features of the larger estuaries, but on a more intimate scale. A waterfall feeds the lagoon from the northernmost stream, and below its silvery threads you will find a place to sit and contemplate the estuary and beyond. From here the track stretches well inland through a patchy forest (also a result of

many burnoffs) of regenerating kanuka and manuka, before regaining the sea at Tonga Quarry (the site of a granite quarry used to furnish stone for a number of prominent buildings and structures in Nelson and Wellington) and the wonderful Onetahuti Beach. Almost certainly somewhere

New Zealand fur seals are regularly seen on rocky headlands and coasts.

on this sandy shore you'll meet a pair of jet-black oystercatchers strutting confidently on their patch and wishing you a speedy departure up the hill to Awaroa estuary.

It is a short stroll from Awaroa hut across to the open beach and the cutting where the ocean enters the enormous estuary. Time and again Awaroa Beach in the vicinity of this cut presents sunsets and sunrises that are profoundly

(Right) Sand ripples across Awaroa estuary at low tide.

The sea brushes against a granite cliff veined and spotted with quartz at Anchorage Bay.

Manuka forest, Separation Point.

Bark Bay waterfall.

more affecting than any you'll see on other Abel Tasman beaches. For at least half an hour at either end of a clear summer's day golden yellow light bathes the estuary's deeply incised sand and shell banks. I suspect the main reasons why this place creates such splendid colours and patterns are found in the combination of its east to west aspect, and its dramatic headlands. Almost all the other beaches face north to south, but at Awaroa the sun's rays are spread down

A grey, rainy day in the Astrolabe Roadstead, looking onto Fisherman Island.

the beach, and shadows are thrown across sand patterns all the more exaggerated by the massive tidal flush that occurs here. The composition of this scene is greatly enhanced by the forested headlands at either end of the bay which form dark waves that divide the impossibly subtle colours of the sand and sky.

The thirteen to fourteen hours between a summer sunrise and sunset at Awaroa can be passed taking long walks down the beach or exploring the estuary at low tide as oystercatchers, white-faced herons and other wading birds feed. On the dunes between beach and estuary you may also find banded dotterel, a small, shy and increasingly threatened bird. Then again, you could pass the time eating cake and drinking real coffee at Awaroa Café at the bay's eastern end.

Having negotiated the route across Awaroa estuary at low tide, the track north of Awaroa sidles slopes that become increasingly scrubby and modified, until there is as much gorse as there is cover of native species. There are, however, some brilliant exceptions to this trend: Goat Bay (reached after ninety minutes) has nikau palms and sprawling rata trees that spray red flowerheads onto the beach; Pukatea walk (another ninety minutes on at Totaranui), a short loop track through dense groves of nikau and tall buttressed pukatea trees; and the arresting muted starkness of the manuka and kanuka forests beyond the final hut at Whariwharangi Bay (three to four hours from Totaranui).

The most compelling reason to walk beyond the road at Totaranui and along the north-eastern corner of the coast to Wainui Inlet (and possibly add another night by staying at the historic homestead hut at Whariwharangi), is to see the granite obelisks at the northern end of Anapai Bay and then head along to Separation Point. For me the entire journey from Marahau was worth it for the windy afternoon I spent at Separation Point, watching gannets scorch past cliffs of wrinkled granite, and seals playing with the exuberance of puppy dogs in the wind-tossed seas.

Spreading boughs of manuka forest at Whariwharangi at the northern end of the national park.

Anchorage Bay stream mouth.

ABEL TASMAN COAST TRACK

Abel Tasman National Park

Length: 50 kilometres.

Time required: 3-5 days.

Nearest centres: Motueka and Takaka.

Best time to walk the track: All year.

Fitness: moderate fitness required.

Information:

Department of Conservation,

Nelson/Marlborough Conservancy,

Private Bag 5, Nelson.

Phone: 03 546 9335. Fax: 03 548 2805.

A Department of Conservation 'Great Walk' the Abel Tasman coast track can be walked at any time of the year. In summer months the track is often crowded, however spring, autumn and winter still offer equable weather and walking conditions, with less people on the track. During summer months bunks at huts must be booked in advance with the Department of Conservation. Hut and camping passes are required. There are numerous camping sites along the route. All huts have toilets, bunks, mattresses and heating. Your own cooking equipment is required. Filtered water supplies are located at all huts and camp sites. There is good public transport to and from the park. Also, water taxis can be hired to deliver walkers to points throughout the coast.

Approximate track times (south to north):

Marahau to Anchorage hut (24 bunks): 3-4 hours.

Anchorage to Bark Bay hut (25 bunks): 3-4 hours.

Bark Bay hut to Awaroa hut (25 bunks): 3 hours.

Awaroa hut to Totaranui (campsite): 2 hours.

Totaranui to Whariwharangi hut (20 bunks): 3 hours.

Whariwharangi hut to Wainui carpark: 1-2 hours.

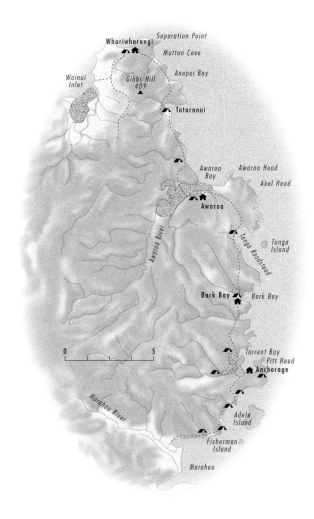

AROUND MT TARANAKI

Circling the cone

Scribed on maps within a circle of disparate green, Egmont National Park is so small and so dominated by the singularity of Mt Taranaki as its cause and centre that really, the only way to enjoy an extended tramping trip here is to walk right around it. In circumnavigating the mountain your choice of tracks will dictate the balance of time spent either in the lowland forest, or higher in the alpine shrub and tussocklands. Whichever direction you walk, circling Taranaki may take between three to five days, perhaps longer if you climb onto the Pouakai Range to the north-west. However there is a certain logic to walking in a clockwise direction from Stratford Mountain House or Dawson Falls on Taranaki's eastern side. In this way you can begin by taking the lower forest route towards and beyond Lake Dive then spiral upwards into subalpine forest and scrub until you reach a climactic high point on the northern flanks (near Humphries Castle, or possibly even the summit) around midday on the last day. From here you can return to the eastern forests via the Curtis Falls track, or

stay high, continuing towards the Stratford Plateau road end and Dawson Falls. Then again, if the weather forecast appears to strongly favour clear weather on the first day or two of the trip, with a likely prospect of rain on days four or five, then I'd recommend you throw all this theory to the wind and head in the opposite direction. What's more, good judgement should lead you to make radical revisions of your route as the tramp unfolds. Whichever way you go, make sure at least one section of your trek is in the lowland forests.

My own walk around Mt Taranaki began on the forest track from the Stratford Mountain House towards Dawson Falls and Lake Dive. What strikes anyone used to the forests of the South Island and other parts of the North is the absence of beech. This can be put down to Taranaki's isolation from a substantial source of beech seed and its long history of volcanic activity that favoured species better able

(Above) Kereru, the native woodpigeon.

96

Reddy-gold hues on Taranaki's north-western flanks above the kamahi/rata forest near Holly hut.

than beech to quickly colonise landscapes obliterated by ice, mud, lava and other volcanic ejecta. On Mt Taranaki the soft green light you would associate with a beech forest is replaced by the harsher and darker reflections from the leaves of kamahi, totara and a variety of other squat forest trees. Any fleeting nostalgia for beech is soon lost along the track as it crosses the innumerable deeply cut side streams radiating from Fanthams Peak. Ferns layer the trackside, and kamahi reaches out over streams like huge inverted, moss-festooned candelabras. On occasions rimu or southern rata erupt from the canopy, while totara covered with the same slimy green mosses as kamahi are found on the ridges. The most compelling colour though in this distinctive forest is the reddy purple glow from the leaves of horopito (*Pseudo-wintera colorata*), which becomes virtually incandescent on late autumn evenings.

In a sense Egmont National Park retains an autumnal feel for much of the year, especially when it's shrouded in mist or rain and you can see out under the squalls to the farms below, or beyond to the ocean shining in the sunlight. The mountain is a rain trap that gathers and raises the long heavy clouds that growl in from the Tasman Sea, causing upwards of 8,000 millimetres of rain to fall a year around the treeline—conditions that are perfect for the park's famed 'goblin forests' of moss-draped, epiphyte-covered trees. Even

(Left) Kamahi forest, Dawson Falls.

after rain there is a residual darkness and dampness in the forest that would swing my mood between joy and melancholy, and from a sense of brimming green fecundity to a feeling that the vegetation was almost too excessive.

The walk to Lake Dive is an immersion in these compelling dark forests and sets the feel of the characteristic

The last steps up to Waiaua Gorge hut.

gully and ridge meandering of all the tracks on the mountain. This modest first afternoon leads to a leisurely tramp on the following day to Waiaua Gorge hut. Descending from Lake Dive hut into the lower forests is a good move (there is the alternative option of a higher track) because, although the track is muddy with lots of up and down over tree roots, the forest more than compensates for these inconveniences. Soon after leaving the lake, altitude is quickly lost and glades of rimu, tawa (*Beilschmiedia tawa*) and mahoe (*Melicytus ramiflorus*) increase in number and the occasional huge rata lifts its scraggling form well above the canopy. With each step to lower elevations the soils become deeper, the clime warmer, and soft-green translucent ferns group in glades beneath an expanding range of podocarp trees such as miro and matai. Gazing into entanglements of supplejack, dark

After a long day, a good book to read, at Waiaua Gorge hut.

labyrinths more confused and complex than that constructed by the Minotaur of Greek mythology, you will despair of finding any classical form. Here is a beauty found only, if at all, in swirling lines of chaos.

At the end of the day the track disappears into a small dark ravine that cuts away from the deeply incised Waiaua River and emerges, at the top of a long aluminium ladder, at Waiaua Gorge hut, high on a lava terrace. In the evening the hut is a superb place to look up at the peak that till now has been hidden all day by the forest. Waiaua Gorge hut is a gem. In fact the park's huts are as good as mountain huts get anywhere, and much better than most. Simply designed, and in the case of Waiaua, decidedly elegant, they were built by people who loved wood and unadorned utilitarian structures. Their placement is well chosen—Lake Dive hut is neatly tucked into the edge of a volcanic dome called the Beehive beside a small mountain lake, while Waiaua's main windows face Taranaki's south-western slopes, which at dusk resonate with lime-green moss, golden tussocks, and the shining grey summit.

Beyond sunset, in the last gasps of daylight, Taranaki seems to hover over everything in a tranquil purple glow. Perhaps the peace of Parihaka (the western Taranaki village where Maori employed non-violent resistance against the

(Right) Lava ridges and bluffs and deeply etched gullies on the south-west slopes of Mt Taranaki. The subsidiary cone, Fanthams Peak, is at right.

Bells Falls, in the upper reaches of the Stony River, near Holly hut.

aggressive land grab by European colonists) was strengthened by the mountain that Parihaka's prophets—Te Whiti and Tohu—so frequently turned to. Te Whiti's plea to end the injustices against his people was grounded in this mountain, the core of their domain, and without meaning to depreciate the context of Te Whiti's famous speech in 1903, we can all hear many levels of meaning in his statement "Ask that mountain, Taranaki saw it all".

From Waiaua Gorge hut the round-the-mountain track sidles to the westernmost aspect of the mountain. Rainfall is highest here and tree trunks massed with kidney ferns also dangle insignificant-looking *Temespterisis* plants, in fact a highly significant species in the evolutionary path towards higher ferns. Beyond Kahui hut your eyes are pulled up and into alpine slopes where long walls of basalt, falling in straight lines or in gentle arcs, appear above the bushline. Strangely symmetrical pyramids of tussock and domes of forest appear, and it becomes evident to even the least geologically inclined that until very recently hot volcanic forces have been at work in this landscape. Taranaki has lain silent since a relatively minor ash fall settled about its upper slopes in 1775, though vulcanologists describe Taranaki not as extinct but dormant, and likely at some time in the future to explode again with perhaps catastrophic force. This may be a discomforting thought, but such events have been occurring on Taranaki for over 120,000 years, in which time the

Little Pyramid, between Kahui and Holly huts.

summit cone has been raised to a height of 2,700 metres, shattered by a series of fiery eruptions and rebuilt to its present elevation. The vast ringplain around Taranaki is tens of metres deep with material from these eruptions, including the hilly mounds of enormous mudflows or lahars that spewed from the crater. North of the mountain, the Pouakai and Kaitake ranges are eroded remnants of ancient volcanoes that in the past two million years rose to similar heights as Taranaki, while outside the park this chain of volcanism is completed by the Sugar Loaf islands and Paritutu Rock at New Plymouth, all that is left of an even earlier volcano.

Holly hut is certainly deserving of a two night stay (or perhaps spend one night at Holly and another at Pouakai hut). Here the light at the end of the day paints glorious hues over the forests, ridges and high summit—a must for a contemplative evening around the hut or out on the Ahukawakawa swamp. The short trip to Stony River and the Bells Falls is also best made in the late afternoon. On the flat just before the track reaches the Stony River is a glade of tall moss-trussed horopito that glows yellow/red in the angled late afternoon light. This same luminescence

Holly hut.

reflects a darker gold resonance off the huge river boulders below Bells Falls, and burnishes the forest dark rusty red on the wander back to the hut. Even if you don't take the side trip across to Pouakai hut it's worth dropping down to Ahukawakawa swamp, a large montane mire that supports a small exceedingly rare divaricating shrub named *Melicytus drucei* which is unique to this area. Here the Stony River meanders through a frost flat of alpine tussocks surrounded by forest-covered lava domes and ridges.

The last day from Holly hut back to the road end is virtually all above the forest except for a delightful interlude at the beginning of the day beside scraggly leatherwood and leaning trunks of kaikawaka (*Libocedrus bidwillii*), a cedar that appears more ancient than the land itself. The track winds around rocky gullies and up and across open spurs that all the while reveal stories of ash showers laid many metres thick during violent cataclysms and sculpted into shape by rivers running from the summit rocks in heavy rainstorms. Amidst this conglomerate of unconsolidated ash and eroded lava are blocky lumps of lava and ash and arching lava ridges and domes. In fact your trip around the mountain is like a geological game of snakes and ladders where you skirt up and down and sometimes slyly around gullies and bluffs, domes and unconsolidated screes. But there are always places, especially on this last day, where the eye tells the tired body to stop and contemplate the

Subalpine shrublands in the lower reaches of Peters Stream near Holly hut. Carrington Ridge is on the left.

Prince of Wales ferns.

conjunction of all these volcanic forms. After a few hours the track enters a series of large gullies, the most active being the Boomerang Slip. Lava bluffs overhang the track towards Dieffenbach Cliffs, while below, ochre-laden creeks suggest the earth is severely fractured and pouring out samples of its rich interior colours.

Beyond Dieffenbach Cliffs, even if the weather is half fine, it's worth taking the high route up the appropriately named Jacobs Ladder to spend the latter part of the day amongst the tussocks and herbfields of the higher slopes. Alpine fields are invigorating places, but this one has a weird surprise in the form of the huge aerial near Tahurangi Lodge,

and the recognition this brings that such structures and ways of the world are omnipresent. It's not that the upper slopes and herbfields aren't superb in themselves, but it is the incongruity of this aerial so high on the mountain that makes the end of this trip so sudden and sobering.

If you take the high route to the Stratford Plateau the track wends its way from Tahurangi Lodge in a gradual descent past Warwicks Castle towards Manganui Ski-field and the road end. The low route, via the Maketawa gorge and the Curtis Falls track, returns you again to Taranaki's dark forests for the last hours across its eastern slopes.

A chaotic tangle of supplejack vines in kamahi forest on the Taungatara Track.

In misty, montane forests, thick mosses hang from distinctive kaikawaka (mountain cedar) trunks long after the trees have died.

AROUND MT TARANAKI

Egmont National Park

Time required: 3-7 days (depending on routes taken).
Nearest centres: New Plymouth, Stratford, Hawera.
Best time to walk the track: November-May.
Fitness: moderate fitness required.

The circuit of Mt Taranaki can be started from one of three road access points within Egmont National Park: North Egmont, Stratford Mountain Motor Lodge/Stratford Plateau, or Dawson Falls. Backpacker style accommodation is available at North Egmont and Dawson Falls. The circuit can be varied to include upper and lower areas of the mountain. All huts on the route described have bunks, mattresses and heating stoves, with the exception of Kahui which does not have heating. Your own cooking equipment, fuel and utensils must be carried. Hut passes are required.

Approximate track times (clockwise direction):
Stratford Mountain House to Dawson Falls via Waingongoro Track: 1 hour.
Dawson Falls to Lake Dive hut (16 bunks) **via Lower Lake Dive Track:** 3-4 hours.
Lake Dive to Waiaua Gorge hut (16 bunks) **via Taungatara Track:** 6 hours.
Waiaua Gorge hut to Holly hut (38 bunks) **via Kahui hut** (6 bunks): 5.5 hours.
Holly hut to Stratford Plateau via Tahurangi Lodge: 4.5 hours.
Stratford Plateau to Stratford Mountain Motor Lodge: 1 hour.

Lower route from Tahurangi Lodge to Stratford Mountain House via Maketawa hut and Curtis Falls Track.
Holly hut to Tahurangi Lodge (privately owned): 3 hours.
Tahurangi Lodge to Maketawa hut (16 bunks) **via Translator Rd:** 1-2 hours.
Maketawa hut to Stratford Mountain Motor Lodge: 3-4 hours.

Information:
North Egmont Visitor Centre,
Egmont Rd, Inglewood.
Phone: 06 756 8710.

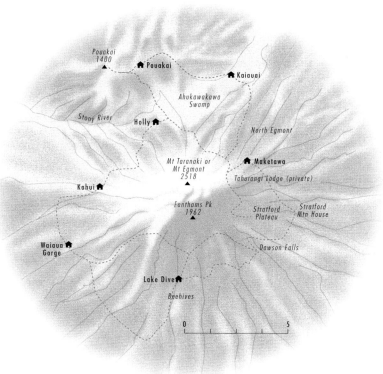

AROUND
THE VOLCANOES

A circuit of Ruapehu and Tongariro

Although there are many captivating landscapes in Tongariro National Park I would return every year even if there was no more to enjoy than the strange beauty of Red Crater. Found on the highest point of the track over Mt Tongariro, Red Crater is a deep cloven void those from Hindu cultures would have little difficulty describing as the genital opening or yoni which invokes the procreative glory of Mother Earth. Should this metaphor seem risqué, imagine instead an ancient forge still in full heat, blood red and dripping silver metal through the black background. I have walked the lip of this extraordinary structure many times and spiralled down shifting reddy-black pumice into the crater's silent centre of collapsed rocks where strange multi-coloured forms blown from the earth carry the pockmarked scars of past eruptions. Surrounded by places where the earth's latent fury steams and regularly explodes from cracks in hot moulded rocks, the centre of Red Crater is a paradox of quiet and peace, a place T.S. Eliot might have called a "still turning point" or a dynamic centre from which the earth's energy emanates. On the crater's eastern flanks, steam and trickling water from a full-blown geothermal cliff feed a brew of chemicals into three emerald-coloured lakes, and above the pumice and the rainbow hues of scoria on the crater's floor is the strange silver-lipped tongue (the forge within the forge) that dominates the south-western corner.

Moving about in surreal places like Red Crater you get the feeling that what was created yesterday could be gone tomorrow, a feeling that is a geological truth on the whole walk around the volcanoes of Tongariro National Park. Unlike any other long walk in New Zealand, this journey immerses you in a milieu of active volcanoes in which heat

(Above) Beech tree in the Mangaturuturu valley.

The northern slopes of Mt Ruapehu.

from the earth radiates to the surface in ways that are both dramatic and subtle. I have chosen to describe a route that starts in the Mangatepopo valley, traverses about half of Mt Tongariro's complex slopes, drops into the Oturere valley then circles around Mt Ruapehu before returning to the national park headquarters at Whakapapa. It is a walk of about six to seven days, but one that can be done in shorter segments as there are tracks out to roads in several places.

The walk up the Mangatepopo valley is bounded in the south at first by the creamy reddish blocks of lava that make up the huge dome of Pukekaikiore, and then by the immense presence of Mt Ngauruhoe. On fine days Ngauruhoe is pitched in perfect symmetry, like a child's tent, black against a blue summer sky, and on stormy days, when all you can glimpse are ascending lines and ridges without apparent end, the mountain seems to take on enormous bulk. Flows of older grey lava are overlapped by the avalanche tracks of knobbly black lava from an eruption of Ngauruhoe in 1954, and it's on combinations of this more recent lava that you cross on the easy, well-trodden path to the South Crater of Mt Tongariro. South Crater is an eerie plateau of orange-yellow clay, somewhat like a salt lake, where pebbles of pumice and lava have been swirled about in S-curves by rain and snowfall. Large volcanic rocks ejected

(Left) On the edge of Tongariro's Red Crater, looking north across the Emerald Lakes towards Blue Lake.

during violent eruptions lie scattered over the crater floor, and late in summer blossoming alpine gentians complete a sense of being in a desert.

From here you can climb in long zigzags up Ngauruhoe, or carry on to Red Crater and circle around to the summit of Tongariro. But there is so much to see I wonder about the wisdom of walking too fast and too far in such places. Past Red Crater and down the Oturere valley you

Mts Ngauruhoe and Tongariro, from the east.

are still on Tongariro, an old and spacious monarch who lords over the landscape, his impressive girth bedecked with exquisite jewels and other finery: the perfect circles of Blue and Emerald lakes, the Te Maari craters, Ketetahi springs and the South, North and Red craters.

Although it's hard to tear yourself away from the centre of Tongariro, the walk down twisting sheets of lava and across the Oturere valley to Oturere hut should not be rushed. One reason is to allow time amongst the strange statue-like blocks that litter the valley's sandy plain, a collection of eccentric lava structures seemingly 'frozen' into shape because they cooled so rapidly.

The journey from Oturere to Waihohonu hut and beyond leads inevitably towards the increasingly drier, windier and psychic whirlpool of the Rangipo Desert. Here and there clumps of beech forest stand uneasily on the desert's edge amongst patches of scrub and lava. The scrub eventually retreats into defensive circles, rather like threatened wagon trains—on the outer margins are a protective golden pallisade of miniature totara trees (*Podocarpus nivalis*) just fifteen centimetres high, next a rank of grey *Rhacomitrium* moss, and massed in the centre are dracophyllums, tall hebes and the occasional mountain toatoa. Over a rise, about forty minutes from Waihohonu hut, is the Rangipo Desert itself, with its sweeps of eroded and deeply gullied ash and pumice, and high ridges stretching through the landscape like long ochre limbs. The wind has smoothed the tops of these mute nude forms and flash floods have etched deep gullies in between; vegetation survives within tussock clumps, or is shunted into prominence upon high pedestals on which the exposed silvery roots of the tawny-barked *Olearia nummulariifolia* grip at whatever they can.

The desert carries many hallmarks of the badlands that it is: constant winds, and whirlwinds of dust tumble things about. Many travellers of deserts talk of the sky as a giant overbearing presence, and so it is in the heart of the Rangipo. A Maori waiata I found researching a previous book on Tongariro carried many of the evocations I have felt in such places: "the stranger humbly offers his heart as food for you". Just before Rangipo hut, the track drops into a barren gorge where the Whangaehu River rushes past carrying its grey brew of chemical-laden waters from Ruapehu's crater lake. After the final climb to the hut you feel as though you have walked into the desert sky. The hut rattles, clouds scuttle around and below, and the cold sets in with the evening.

Six months after Mt Ruapehu erupted in July 1996, much of the Rangipo was covered in a taut grey skin of water-logged ash that cracked and emitted a stinking sulphurous smell from under my feet as I walked along. This of course is part of the central story of the park, in which the earth has erupted and turned itself inside out many times, though no-one has ever witnessed the terrifying scale and force of the largest eruptions said to have occurred over the past hundreds of thousands of years. Though spectacular, the recent eruptions were an extremely minor episode in a long and violent geological history. Numerous volcanoes have stood on this landscape, and Ruapehu and Mt Tongariro are simply the latest of these, relatively young (20,000 years) 'strato-volcanoes' comprised of composite

The Rangipo Desert near the Whangaehu valley; Mt Ngauruhoe on the horizon.

*The northern slopes of Mt Ruapehu from National Park, with the forested ridge
from Hauhungatahi Peak in the foreground.*

cones and multiple layers of ash, scoria and lava.

Not far along the track to Mangaehuehu hut the desert sandscape merges into rockfields where millions of evenly sized lava boulders lie strewn across the ashy expanse. This monochromatic world reaches its apogee in the sweeping valley of the Wahianoa River, beyond which the route slowly creeps past the mountain's rainshadow and squat plants like the red and sharply leaved *Dracophyllum recurvum*, small white-flowering ourisias and the eyebright *Euphrasia cuneata* assert their life and colours. The colours of the land become even stronger and more varied when mountain beech trees draped in white lichen enfold you in their comforting greenness for the first time in three to four days. One hour on in a clearing that offers views of sunsets shining on the huge bulk of Ruapehu, is Mangaehuehu hut . If Ngauruhoe's perfect symmetry can be compared to a child's tent, then the sight of Ruapehu from here is of a near perfect big top with three central apexes: the peaks of Girdlestone, Tahurangi and Paretetaitonga.

To reach Mangaturuturu hut involves a slightly disorientating walk up the Turoa ski-field road. People drive by at a completely different pace, no doubt considerably cleaner

Mangaturuturu Stream.

Volcanic dyke and lava bombs on the floor of Red Crater, Mt Tongariro.

than you after four or five days walking, and you can but envy their hampers of fresh food and chilled drinks. After an hour the track resumes and sidles into an amphitheatre of lava bluffs with numerous waterfalls and cascades. I explored here for several hours, then wandered down to the comfortable and quaint Mangaturuturu hut built by the Wanganui Tramping Club in 1958, with its fourteen-frame window facing the mountain's summit.

Once safely over the Mangaturuturu River the track to Whakapapa climbs through irregular boulders under groves of old, squat beech forest above a lava escarpment on the edge of the valley, and past the dark and brooding waters of Lake Surprise. Although it may not seem a very long way on the map from Mangaturuturu hut to Whakapapa, the day is a reasonably long one on an exposed mountain face. After five or six hours the landscape opens out and the trail moves across the headwaters of the Whakapapaiti River, returning you once again to a road, civilisation and the national park's headquarters at Whakapapa Village.

The June 1996 eruption of Mt Ruapehu.

Emerald Lake, Mt Tongariro.
(Left) A beech grove on the track near Mangaehuehu hut.

Lava bombs on the Rangipo Desert.

AROUND THE VOLCANOES

Tongariro National Park

Time required: 4-6 days.
Nearest centre: Whakapapa Village.
Best time to walk: November to April.
Fitness: Moderate fitness required.

The circuit of the Tongariro volcanoes is a varied forest and alpine walk through a range of volcanic landforms along well-marked, though often quite exposed, tracks. In bad weather, sections of this route (over Mt Tongariro and on the Rangipo Desert) may be impossible due to rain, poor visibility and even snow. Good equipment is essential. Huts have bunks, stoves for heating, and water supplies and toilets. Your own cooking equipment must be carried. Camping is allowed outside most huts. Whakapapa Village on the northern slopes of Mt Ruapehu has accommodation from campsites to luxury accommodation, visitor information services, and a general store. Shuttle services can be arranged from here for those wanting to be dropped off at points around the park.

Approximate Track Times (clockwise direction):
Whakapapa Village to Mangatepopo hut
(24 bunks): 3-4 hours.
Mangatepopo hut to Oturere hut
(23 bunks): 5-6 hours.
Oturere hut to Waihohonu hut
(22 bunks): 2-3 hours.
Waihohonu hut to Rangipo hut
(24 bunks): 4-5 hours.
Rangipo hut to Mangaehuehu hut
(23 bunks): 5-6 hours.
Mangaehuehu hut to Mangaturuturu hut
(16 bunks): 5-6 hours.

Mangaturuturu hut to Whakapapaiti hut (24 bunks): 6 hours.
Whakapapaiti hut to Whakapapa Village: 2-3 hours.

Information:

Whakapapa Field Centre,
Department of Conservation,
Private Bag, Mt Ruapehu.
Phone: 07 892 3729.
Fax: 07 892 3814.

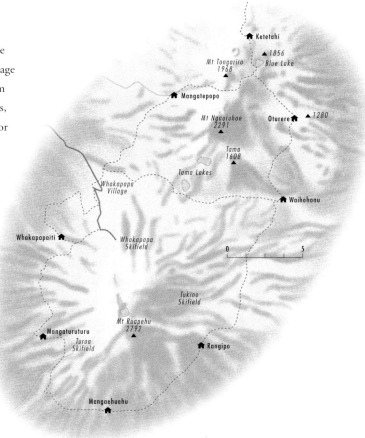

THE CIRCUIT OF
LAKE WAIKAREMOANA

Secret forests and waters of Te Urewera

Despite the dusty road that splits the huge Urewera wilderness, there remains a sense of 'other-worldliness' about Te Urewera National Park. In this largest of all the fragments of North Island forest, the author Katherine Mansfield also sensed a mood when she wrote "it is all so gigantic and tragic—and even in the bright sunlight it is so passionately secret". The Tuhoe and neighbouring iwi, who lived in these ranges for hundreds of years before Pakeha came, discovered its hallowed places and secrets, and named its rivers, lakes, forests and mountain ranges. So powerfully does the land speak that Tuhoe trace their ancestry to the coupling of the mist maiden Hine-pukoho-rangi, and the mountain Te Maunga, a myth from which comes the name 'Children of the Mist', as Tuhoe are also known. Tuhoe alone can recount these mysteries should you wish to discover more about them, though glimpses of their relationship with the land are revealed in Elsdon Best's

monographs on the Tuhoe and Judith Binney's works on Tuhoe prophets Rua Kenana and Te Kooti, or by searching into the huge Colin McCahon painting at the national park visitor centre. But it is better, if chance or grace allows it, to speak directly to and learn from the Tuhoe, who still live near the sacred centres of their land. No matter from where our myths and unconscious calls emanate, Lake Waikaremoana and Te Ure-wera's forests have a deep resonance for all who go to them. Many now make the journey around Lake Waikaremoana, which from on high appears gangly and long-fingered, an aquamarine starfish held by an enveloping clasp of forest. The popular myth describing the lake's creation tells the tragic story of Haumapahia, a female taniwha or mythical water monster at odds with her father's will, desperately thrashing through

(Above) Panekiri hut. (Right) Lake Waikaremoana from Panekiri Bluff.

Korokoro Falls, a short distance up Korokorowhaitiri Stream from the lake track.

the land by night and gouging the enclosing hillsides in her attempts to find a way to the ocean, knowing that daylight would turn her to stone. Water filled the places where she clawed at the hillsides and the lake was created, and although Haumapahia lost her struggles when daylight came, the lake's many bays and indentations are reminders of her tragic struggle. Certainly the land shows no easy ways to orientate and get one's bearings because no single mountain peak rises above the forest and no central river dominates; it's just a series of sharp ridges and deep valleys one upon another spiralling out from the lake. In fact the only interruption from the forest blanket is Panekiri Bluff, the severe rock escarpment on the lake's southern shores.

Panekiri Bluff rises 600 metres from the lake, its great walls glowing a golden pallor on sunny days, and wreathed in mist and cloud when it rains. Perched high on these bluffs sits Panekiri hut, a grand viewpoint over a superb wilderness. For some it is near the end and for others just the start of the circumnavigation of Waikaremoana. Below lies the lake and a view of water and forest ridges interlapping blue on blue, while beyond, more ethereal blues denote ridges westward to the horizon. I once stood outside looking west when a German backpacker interrupted my quiet with the simple truism: "everywhere you look is forest". In the peace of such high places, where no water runs except for the rain and the mist gathering on trees, and no sound disturbs ex-

The view north-west across the Whareama Range into Wairaumoana (Wairau Arm) of Lake Waikaremoana, from Bald Knob on the Panekiri Range.

cept the tuneless whistling of the wind, you can look upon a view without the imprint of human interference and find spoken words remarkably unnecessary.

Because many people look at Panekiri Bluff seduced by the prospects of wonderful morning and evening views (and perhaps fearful of the hard grunt from the lake to the top) they set out to walk Waikaremoana clockwise, as most guidebooks suggest. However there is no method to the madness of walking straight up a bluff on the first day. It is much better to engage the road- or water-taxi to the Hopuruahine entrance and take on the hill-climb on the last day after you have eaten your way through some of your pack's

load and worked a few muscles into shape.

The walk around Lake Waikaremoana is along a forty-six kilometre track, largely in excellent condition, that can be dawdled in four days and easily tramped in three. From the Hopuruahine entrance the first five hours between Whanganui hut and Tapuaenui campsite to Te Puna hut introduces you to the three types of forest that you'll encounter off and on over the next few days: a resplendent mature rimu/tawa forest, largely in the gullies; regenerating manuka/tree fern patches, usually closer to the water's edge (resulting from new surfaces exposed in 1946 when hydro development lowered the lake's level by five metres), and on the drier ridges and faces is the more open sooty-barked hard beech and mingimingi (*Leucopogon fasciculata*) forest. It's a varied forest that throws up some wonderfully buttressed beech trees, and perhaps because of its overall size and variety and the insects that gather over the water's edge, seems particularly rich in birdlife. If you're lucky you'll hear and see kaka and parakeet, and at night hear moreporks calling dolefully for "more pork" and screeching North Island brown kiwi. Common birds are abundant: pigeons, paradise ducks, whiteheads, riflemen, grey warblers, tomtits, fantails and silvereyes. What you almost definitely won't see (and won't be sensitive enough to hear) are the rare nocturnal long-tailed and short-tailed bats that roost in the boles of ancient trees.

Marauiti hut, three hours walk from Te Puna hut, is pleasantly sited beside a finger of water where the broad Marauiti river flows gently into the lake at Marauiti Bay. The hut's red roof and expansive cream lounge with large windows is a convivial place even on the greyest of days,

Views from Panekiri Bluff: east along the Panekiri Range (left), and across Lake Waikaremoana.

and if the mosquitoes and sandflies aren't too bad, its sheltered porch is a good place for taking in the view while contemplating a pasta dinner.

The track beyond Marauiti heads over a beech-covered spur with strongly buttressed trees, along with many tawa and a few scattered rimu. Then it leads down into one of Waikaremoana's typically small and grassy lakeside flats, this one at Maraunui Bay. Here there are groves of manuka

129

and grassy banks beside the creek and lakeside. A virtue of this lake walk for those who find fitness a challenge is that nowhere is too far from places where one can quietly meditate upon the view and rest tired muscles. And in such vein, although it may seem like an unnecessary uphill diversion late in the afternoon to reach Korokoro Falls (and also make Waiopaoa hut that evening), the falls are definitely worth the effort. They are reached by an enchanting ridge track through a lush forest of tanekaha (*Phyllocladus trichomanoides*), the large-leaved *Dracophyllum traversii* and stunted forms of beech trees standing out from the dense, twirling groves of tawa. Below the track the Korokorowhaitiri Stream gives sculptural expression to blocks of limestone that have been progressively rolled down the creekbed.

A soldier's name carved on the walls of the military redoubt at Sandy Bay that was used by Government forces in their battles with Te Kooti Rikirangi, an outstanding Maori warrior leader.

The smallish stream won't prepare you for the size of the waterfall, which is sighted through an envelope of large beech trees festooned in kidney ferns. In rain, water fills the face of the fall, forming a large rectangular twenty metre high curtain of water. By climbing carefully down on the left (when you look towards the falls), you can walk on a scalloped, gently sloping papa (mudstone) shelf amongst several huge boulders—sentinels to the falls themselves. Because papa is so consistent in constitution, and so water-soluble, it erodes like limestone, leaving sculpted blocks of harder rocks resting on flat surfaces and weir-like drops covered with gentle flows of water.

The next day's climb from Waiapaoa to Panekiri hut follows a series of obvious ridge lines for the first two hours, before zigzagging between bluffs to gain the Panekiri Range, and then the hut after a further hour-and-a-half of easy wandering. From above the zigzag, silver beech gives way to mountain beech, and mountain totara replaces tawa as the dominant understorey layer. On these steeper slopes the long plank-like black buttresses of beech trees form sheets that slice into the dark earth. The range is often covered in misty clouds, even when the weather is clear below. It is at these times that the mosses and lichens blanketing the trees and branches stand out in swollen clumps, giving the impression that every tree is ancient.

After an evening and early morning at Panekiri hut

Mist hangs in beech forest on the Panekiri Range.

Korokorowhaitiri Stream below Korokoro Falls.

the route down the Panekiri Range to complete the circle at the road end is essentially a reversal of the day before, starting with the 'ancient' mist forest and descending through tawa groves to the great lake. There are several lookouts on this descent that not only give magnificent views, but also lead your thoughts back 2,200 years when a huge landslip detached from the Ngamoko Range (directly north of the lake's exit) and blocked the Waikaretaheke River, allowing the waters of Waikaremoana to fill up. This is the geological explanation of Waikaremoana, a story that, like Maori myths and the Pakeha's sense of mystery, lies hidden under a forest mantle, but which still reverberates in the unconscious like a passionate secret.

(Right) Beech tree detail on the trail between Waiopaoa hut and Korokorowhaitiri Bay.

LAKE WAIKAREMOANA TRACK

Te Urewera National Park

Length: 46 kilometres.

Time required: 3-4 days.

Nearest town: Wairoa.

Best time to walk the track: November-April.

Fitness: moderate fitness required.

The Lake Waikaremoana track is a Department of Conservation 'Great Walk'. It is well constructed and has several large huts supplied with bunks, mattresses and heating. You need to take your own cooking stoves and fuel. There are several campsites along the track though camping is not permitted on the Panekiri Range (including next to Panekiri hut). Hut and camping passes are required. The track can be reached from Wairoa in the east, and from the Central North Island, west of the lake. Bus transport is available from major centres.

Approximate walking times
(anticlockwise direction from Hopuruahine track entrance.
The track can be walked in either direction):

Hopuruahine Landing to Whanganui hut (18 bunks): 3 hours.

Whanganui hut to Te Puna hut (18 bunks): 2 hours.

Te Puna hut to Marauiti hut (18 bunks): 3 hours.

Maruiti hut to Waiopaoa hut (22 bunks): 4-5 hours.

Waiopaoa hut to Panekiri hut (22 bunks): 3.5-4.5 hours.

Panekiri hut to Onepoto track entrance: 3-4 hours.

Information:

Department of Conservation,
Aniwaniwa Visitor Centre,
Te Urewera National Park,
Private Bag 2213, Wairoa.
Phone and fax: 06 837 3803.

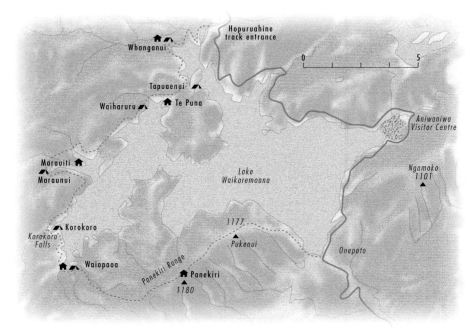

TRAMPING IN NEW ZEALAND

The walks in this book are along tracks maintained by the Department of Conservation (DoC). Most (the exception being the north-west circuit of Stewart Island) are along well-constructed tracks that are easy to follow, with major obstacles like rivers safely bridged. Several of these tracks are designated 'Great Walks' on which a higher standard of track construction and/or facilities can be expected. Hut passes are required for all huts, and these can be purchased from DoC field centres and information centres; in some cases passes are also required for campsites.

The popularity of the Milford and Routeburn tracks is such that bunk space in huts must be booked ahead of your walk during the summer months. At the time of writing a booking system is likely to be introduced in the near future for Abel Tasman coast track and Heaphy track facilities. On other walks sleeping space is claimed on a first-come, first-served basis. Unless the track you're on has booked accommodation, carrying a tent during summer is a good idea, allowing you the opportunity to camp in places away from huts and people. On most of these walks you will need to carry your own cooking equipment and utensils, and even where gas is supplied for cooking, having your own cooker will mean an early dinner in a crowded hut. Guided walks are available on the Milford, Routeburn and Abel Tasman tracks. Contact the Department of Conservation for information on these opportunities.

When should you go? The months of summer, between December and March, are obviously the best because of the warmer temperatures, longer daylight hours, and generally drier conditions underfoot. But spring and autumn can also provide good walking conditions, and there are often fewer people on the tracks. For several months during winter, the Kepler, Milford and Routeburn may be impassable because of snow or high avalanche danger. The Heaphy track is occasionally closed by snow but is often walked in winter. The circuits of Mt Taranaki and Ruapehu are subject to snow on higher sections and are more marginal winter walks. However, the Abel Tasman coast track and Lake Waikaremoana circuit are both feasible through winter months, and although the nights may be cold, temperatures can also be pleasant without being overly hot.

The success of your walk will hinge on your preparation—being physically fit and able to carry a pack, your route research, having appropriate equipment, and being ready for bad weather or accidents. Talk to others who have done the walk. Get up-to-date information about track conditions from Department of Conservation staff. DoC has maps and brochures available for all of these tracks, and there are many well-researched tramping guides available (see page 136) that provide more information than is possible in a book of this nature.

One of the most unpredictable factors in the back country is the weather. All of these routes are susceptible to bad weather, flooded rivers, slips, snow and high winds. To be prepared for the inevitable downpour, good storm clothing and strong footwear is essential for all these walks. 'Reading' weather in the mountains comes with experience, but perhaps the soundest advice is to be conservative in your decision making about whether to carry on. Listen to the advice of hut wardens and other walkers, and if you are out in bad weather, be wary of hypothermia amongst members of your party (hypothermia is a dangerous cooling of the core body temperature that can occur with little warning during exposure to cold weather, and untreated, leads to death). Don't forget to take a sunhat, and carry sunscreen and insect repellent in your first aid kit.

EQUIPMENT FOR WILDERNESS PHOTOGRAPHY

There is a very real tension in photography on multi-day walks. It's a practical problem of deciding how much extra equipment to carry in a pack that is already full of heavy essential gear. My priority is to carry lots of film, a light tripod, an umbrella and a 35 mm SLR camera with standard lenses: (50 mm) and a medium wide-angle (35 mm). To my way of thinking the tripod is as important as the camera, as many moody shots are taken in low light in the forest or at the ends of each day.

If I am able to add more weight to my pack I take a small telephoto lens (135 mm or 180 mm) and a wider-angle lens such as a 28 mm. To get high quality photos (such as the dark forest interiors on pages 12 and 22) I use a much heavier medium-format camera. With this camera I carry three lenses: one standard and two wide-angled. I always carry spare batteries for both camera and flash units. Everyone has their own favourite films (or if they don't they should). Mine are 'professional' Kodachrome 64 in 35 mm, and Ektachrome EPR in medium format (120 mm). If you want to make prints for your photo album or for enlargement and display, then negative film is best, whereas, if you hope to submit your photographs for publication or have slide shows, then transparency film is best.

RECOMMENDED READING

Bishop, Nic. *Natural History of New Zealand*. Hodder & Stoughton, Auckland, 1992.

Burton, R. & Atkinson, M. *A Tramper's Guide to New Zealand's National Parks*. Revised edition, Reed Publishing, Auckland, due 1998.

Department of Conservation guides: a series of pamphlets for most of the popular walking tracks prepared by the Department of Conservation.

Forsyth, J., Turnbull, I., Lee, B. & Beecroft, Gary. *A Guide to the Kepler Track*. John McIndoe in association with DSIR, Dunedin, 1991.

Mark, A. F. & Adams, Nancy M. *New Zealand Alpine Plants*. Reed Publishing, Auckland, 1979.

Pickering, Mark. *101 Great Tramps in New Zealand*. Reed New Zealand, Auckland.

Salmon, J. T. *Native Trees of New Zealand*. Heinemann Reed, Auckland, 1990.

Shaw, Derek. *North West Nelson Tramping Guide*. Nikau Press, Nelson, 1991.

Stevens, Graeme. *New Zealand Adrift*. A. H. & A .W. Reed, Auckland, 1980.

Thornton, Jocelyn. *Field Guide to New Zealand Geology*. Reed Methuen, Auckland, 1985.

Webb, C., et al. *Flowering Plants of New Zealand*. DSIR Botany, with Caxton Press, Christchurch, 1990.